Count It All Joy

Reflections on Building Community

Count It All Joy

Reflections on Building Community

Edited by Leonard M. Young

Herald Publishing House
Independence, Missouri

Congregational Services Division
Reorganized Church of Jesus Christ of Latter Day Saints

Herald Publishing House
Independence, Missouri

Printed in the United States of America

Library of Congress Cataloging in Publication Data
Count it all joy : reflections on building community / Leonard M. Young, editor.
p. cm.
Includes bibliographical references and index.
ISBN 0-8309-0724-6
1. Reorganized Church of Jesus Christ of Latter Day Saints—Membership. 2. Church renewal—RLDS Church. 3. Joy—Religious aspects. I. Young, Leonard M., 1950–
BX8675.C68 1996 95-48377
289.3'33—dc20 CIP

99 98 97 96 1 2 3 4 12-059015

Table of Contents

Preface

Ever since the Communities of Joy emphasis was launched in 1994, individuals have been asking how the concept of a relational church can be lived out. Most commonly this question revolves around the differences between program-focused and relationship-focused congregational life. At the core of the distinction between these two approaches to ministry is the belief that community building is a central calling of the church.

This book contains articles on how to infuse the spirit of community into congregational life. Each is written by a different author who brings a unique perspective to the discussion. The focus of these articles is on taking the discussion of the church's Communities of Joy emphasis to a deeper and more personal level.

The authors were encouraged to write from personal experience and to explore the theological and practical aspects of how a Community of Joy can be built. The hope is that this will be a "heart trip and not just a head trip" for those who read and study the book.

The epistle of James begins with the words, "My brothers and sisters, whenever you face trials of any kind, count it all joy . . ." (James 1:2). The writer makes this strange statement in the face of all the difficulties facing the fledgling first-century Christian Church. Yet through all their difficulties the joy of the gospel was central to the life of their faith community.

Today we need to ask how it can be possible to acknowledge the realities of life–as difficult as they may be–and still celebrate life as a gift from God. The answer is found in the joy that comes from the relationships we have with others and with God. Joy is a fruit of the Spirit and cannot be manufactured or programmed. Instead, joy is a by-product of the development of true community among those who have committed themselves to a life based on gospel principles. Joy arises as our community life is anchored to a faith in God's purposes being fulfilled and linked to the life of the Spirit.

This book is offered to the church in the hope that as we all struggle with new faith issues and with old issues in new forms, we may be blessed by the assurance that nothing can separate us from each other and the work to which we have been called (paraphrase Doctrine and Covenants 122:17b) if the spirit of true community is at the heart of our congregational life.

Leonard M. Young

Introduction

Howard S. Sheehy Jr.

At the beginning of the 1990 World Conference, Florine's father passed away and the guests in our home found it necessary to "pitch in" with meal preparations and other household chores while Florine gave some assistance and comfort to her mother. One day toward the end of her stay with us, Celia Roddis, a priest from the Sutton-in-Ashfield Branch in England, was drying the dishes while I "washed up." We were both quiet, lost in our own thoughts, when Celia suddenly said, "When I get home things are going to be different." I was not quite sure how to take her comment. Was it related to her home; her husband's participation in "housework"? Perhaps it was a statement about her role in the Aaronic priesthood and the program of the church. Whatever, it was a very clear statement of commitment. I do not question that for Celia, *things* are different.

It was about that same time that I began to think about where the church would go ministerially when the Temple was completed and the "Faith To Grow" program had run its course. I knew we would be depending on a new generation of leaders and that by the mid-nineties, many of our smaller congregations would be struggling for survival.

Over the next four years, we did considerable planning with young adults and with two different headquarters/field committees. We announced the Communities of Joy emphasis at the 1994

[*Editor's Note:* This introduction is based on a presentation made by President Howard S. Sheehy Jr. at the 1995 Aaronic Priesthood Event. It has been adapted for use as the introduction to this book because of its timely nature and message.]

World Conference. It is the product of many gifted, creative people who truly were concerned that the church needed to shift from being struggling congregations to what we envisioned as communities of joy.

At the 1994 World Conference in his sermon during the Monday evening Communities of Joy service, Leonard Young repeated dramatically a phrase contained in his book: "The day of the program-focused church is in twilight; the day of the relational church is beginning to dawn."[1] This declaration was picked up in the video that was used throughout the church for the Communities of Joy launches.

Since that time many people have asked me, "What does that mean? What is the difference between a program-focused church and a relational church?"

In brief, I would say that a programmatic church views the church's task as the conducting of events. It bases its life on what some call straight-line thinking, or cause and effect planning. That is, if we do *this*, we can make *that* happen. It is a little like what Lyle Schaller refers to as starting with our own agenda. We know what we want to do and we believe that this is the way to accomplish it. So to the best of our ability, through the familiar patterns of our church life, we have Sunday morning worship, mid-week prayer services, church school classes, youth activities, business meetings, district/stake conferences, etc.

In this model of congregational life, we have all had our assignments to arrange chairs, give a talk, clean up, encourage participation, offer a prayer, prepare or serve Communion, conduct a family visit, and so on. That way of looking at congregational life is very familiar to us, and in some measure this view has defined our "ministry." Frequently our training programs revolve around developing the skills and procedures necessary to do these tasks well.

The relational church, on the other hand, is based on the idea that the local congregation is a system. All the elements that make up a congregation interact and mutually influence one another and we are influenced constantly by the response people give to our ministry. There is considerable research to suggest that congregations do indeed function like families. We belong to one another. To understand the local church, we do not look at the structure of congregational offices and the duties of each. Instead, we must look at the "whole" and the emotional process that holds it together. It is perhaps from this notion that the apostle Paul refers to the church more than thirty times in the New Testament as the body of Christ with Christ at the head.[2]

The body concept identifies the church as a systemic entity made up of many different parts with varied purposes and characteristics. Tex Sample would say, this is where we "pitch tent." This is not a church we attend; it is where we live out our lives. It is a group of people, centered on the gospel, with emotional commitments that create bonding.

To move from being a programmatic church to a relational church involves more than incremental change. It is not a matter of just doing the same things we have been doing but trying to do them better. If we keep doing the same thing, we are going to get the same results. We will need to make a transformational change.

A community of joy is very different from a struggling congregation. What we are talking about is a new vision for congregational life. We are, and will for some time, experience some confusion about this. It is easy to fall back into familiar patterns, but if we continue to explore the meaning of the local church as a family system we will begin to see with new eyes some remarkable new understandings.

Stewardship 2000 is an interesting example of how this can happen. In those places where Stewardship 2000 is seen in a programmatic manner, as a way to increase church income, it is not doing well. Some would say it has failed. But where Stewardship 2000 is seen as a system to create financial stability in the homes of our people, in our local churches, and at the World Church level, it is very successful.

Paul Dietterich of the Center for Parish Development in Chicago suggests that if we want to engage in the kind of transformational change that will move our congregations from being program-centered to person-centered, there are several basic assumptions that have to change. He is referring to the concept of the local congregation as

- a personal sanctuary,
- society's chaplain,
- a functional guide to personal belief and morality, or
- an organization directed by professional clergy with members as consumers.

Such concepts need to be replaced by the following biblical understandings of the congregation:

1. a family through which God is calling all peoples to be transformed into the people of God;
2. a new paradigm, a contrast society, that demonstrates a different way of being a society;
3. a system where the resources, practices, and services cultivate a new people who learn and practice togetherness;
4. a community of disciples who participate in the new life of the Spirit, and
5. a fellowship in which its life and practice is centered on its mission as the community embodies and announces God's transforming power.[3]

Sometimes I marvel at how prophetic the Restoration movement really is. The concept of church as a community has been with us from our earliest of days.We have had a tendency at times to look at others and think, if we could just be like them. In a day when the survival of churches in general is being questioned, the apparent solution appears to favor our direction of smaller churches with community awareness and member/ministers. I have found myself longing to have our congregations become "full-service" churches and wondered if full-time, professional pastors would not be the answer for us. But I am coming to understand that such thinking comes out of a programmatic church orientation.

From time to time, those from the "outside" like Tex Sample and Lyle Schaller remind us to be faithful to who we are. We need to hear that! We already know how to have small churches and how to use member/ministers. Let's celebrate that knowledge and let it lead us as we envision the future to which God is calling us individually and as congregations.

The movement away from being a program church toward being a relational church will not be an easy journey. In the relational church problems still exist and there will be anxiety. Such pain exists in all relational systems. And it is at this point that our congregations are called to minister.

When we think of the congregation as a family that is constantly engaged in an emotional process it is no wonder we find ourselves confronted with serious personal concerns.

In a typical congregation of 100 people, you might find the following pastoral care issues over a several-year period:

16 - loss of a job
10 - economic woes
5 - business upheaval
4 - bankruptcy
10 - grief or anger related to a former pastor
6 - transferred membership after experiencing discord in previous congregation
8 - major life crises
7 - alcoholism
13 - marital strife
10 - unhappiness with spouse
8 - divorce
4 - death of spouse
6 - serious accidents
6 - pregnant or sexually active teenager
5 - child left home
6 - death of a child
4 - child with social adjustment, substance abuse or academic difficulties
7 - tension in extended family
8 - illness or death of a parent
6 - relocation of a family.[4]

Pearl Bailey, the American singer and tireless charitable volunteer, says, "My husband said to me, 'Honey, you worry too much about people.' I said, 'I don't worry–I care.'"

Here is another transformational change–converting worrying into caring, or as the apostle Paul said, "As we have opportunity, let us do good to all ... especially those who are of the household of faith" (Galatians 6:10).

The emotional processes that will require the focused ministry of congregations will likely be in the areas of

- anxiety and reactive behavior,
- the tension between separateness and closeness,
- the balance between stability and change, and
- the need for clarity and forthrightness tempered by compassion and sympathy.

When I was called to the office of priest, my grandfather wrote me a letter. He said, "Be the best priest you can be; don't be concerned about what others are doing." I was reminded of that advice as I read a list of health-influencing suggestions for ministers who are charged with the health of the congregational family.

Peter Steinke admonishes us:

Focus on self, not others
Focus on strength not weakness
Focus on process not content
Focus on challenge not comfort
Focus on integrity not unity
Focus on system not symptom
Focus on direction not condition[5]

In our proclamation of Jesus Christ, we must be about sustaining and supporting the communities of joy, hope, love, and peace that we call our congregations. In the midst of the struggles of daily life and with the challenge to create such communities, the call to your congregation is to keep your ministry focused on what you are becoming, on what God is calling you to be. You are the stewards of your congregation's vision and the creators of your own future.

This book is about the struggle to be a relational church. The various chapters discuss what it means to be a holistic system that is concerned with not only "head trips, but heart trips" as well. As you read, ask yourself how you can foster a stronger relational orientation in your congregation. As you do so, the community of joy which in many congregations is lying just beneath the surface will begin to shine through.

My friend from England told me, "Things are going to be different." I hope so. For her, for you, and for your congregation.

Notes

1. Leonard M. Young, *Communities of Joy* (Independence, Missouri: Herald House, 1994), 25.
2. Peter L. Steinke, *How Your Church Family Works: Understanding Congregations as Emotional Systems* (Washington, D.C.: The Alban Institute, 1993). The author is indebted to Peter Steinke for the broad development of the church as an emotional process.
3. Paul M. Dietterich, "Why Incremental Changes Won't Work," *Transformation*, The Center for Parish Development.
4. Peter L. Steinke, 46–47.
5. Ibid., 109.

1

Expressing Giftedness

Margaret A. "Peggy" Young

When we moved I was burned out. I needed a break. And for the first time I felt OK about taking one. We were finally in a relatively large congregation with many gifted people. If I sat back on the sidelines for a while this congregation would continue to function just fine. I could relax and be ministered to for a change.

But an unexpected development occurred. Before long, I was feeling spiritually empty. I experienced one of the truths of giftedness: those offering gifts are blessed as much as those receiving them. Yes, my congregation was getting along fine without me, but I was depriving myself and the church of the full measure of God's blessings.

I found myself smack in the middle of something I truly believed would never happen to me. I've been having my mid-life crisis. The predominant question on my mind for the last three years has been, "What am I supposed to do with my life?"

I've always believed there was a purpose for my life, that there were things I was meant to accomplish. And that if I sought God's guidance, I would be led to activities that would impel me down the right path. Until three years ago, I thought that was happening in my life. So why was I in the middle of a crisis?

I sought guidance from many sources in an effort to discover what's been wrong. From mental health professionals who literally saved my life, I discovered that part of my problem was a lack of balance. So I cut out a lot of activity that was hindering my availability to my family and keeping me from pursuits like meditation and inspirational reading. Things improved, but I still felt so tender. Would I ever heal? Would I ever feel whole again?

I felt like the son in Jesus' "prodigal son" parable. But it wasn't the prodigal I identified with; it was the older son who stayed home. Kent Groff's interpretation of this parable in his book, *Active Spirituality: A Guide for Seekers and Ministers*,[1] helped me see another way I was lost.

The prodigal son and the older, perfectionist son were both lost. The prodigal finally realized this when he was reduced to tending pigs. His wasteful extravagance had broken him. His pain was of sadness and regret. This pain caused him to recognize that something was wrong and impelled him on the journey homeward.

The perfectionist was broken, too. When he realized that his father was throwing a party for the younger brother who had squandered his inheritance, he was furious. His anger tells us that he is not totally satisfied with the choices he made for his life. If he were, he would be as happy as his father to see the prodigal back home. But he is not happy. He is full of resentment. We can only deduce why.

I like Groff's suggestion that the perfectionist resents the prodigal for doing exactly what he wanted to do, which implies that the perfectionist has not done some of the things he really wanted to. He was a dutiful son. He did what he assumed he was supposed to do, what was expected of him as the eldest child. He probably wouldn't have wanted to go off with his inheritance as the prodigal did, but there must have been a lot of self-sacrifice to fulfill what he thought was expected of him.

The big difference between the prodigal son and the perfectionist son was that one asked for what he wanted and the other did not. The prodigal asked for what he wanted—twice. And both times he got more than he asked for. The perfectionist probably assumed that some of the things he wanted weren't appropriate and kept silent. So what he got was a lot of resentment. As with his prodigal brother, his pain was a call to recognize that something was wrong and allow it to impel him on a journey homeward. For him, "being home" was not a physical, geographic thing. It was a matter of accepting the father's willingness to allow him to be the person he really wanted to be.

For me, my pain was also a call to recognize that something was wrong. I found myself in the same predicament as the perfectionist—full of resentment for filling my life with so much activity, which I assumed was expected of me, that there wasn't time for the things I really wanted to do, and felt called to do. Just as the perfectionist son, I was broken by too much self-sacrifice. As Groff puts it, I, too, had "wasted my gifts–by failing to claim them!"[2]

I am grateful to all the people–relatives, loved ones, professionals–who helped me face my pain and allow it to impel me on my own journey homeward. The "home" I seek is a place where I am loved and accepted for who I am and what I want to be. And I am discovering that "who I am" is best known through the identification and expression of my gifts. As I am able to do this, my life fills with joy.

Another important source of guidance affirms that this is true for every person. That source is scripture. Ephesians 4:8 reads: "When he [Christ] ascended up on high, he led captivity captive, and gave gifts unto [all]." The writer is quoting from Psalm 68:18. However, the psalm says "*receiving* gifts among [all]," but in Ephesians it is changed to "*gave* gifts to [all]." William Barclay explains this as an illustration of the difference between the Old Testament understanding that a jealous, conquering God *demands and receives* gifts from people, and the New Testament understanding that a loving God pours out his love by *giving* gifts. That which holds us captive, is taken captive by Christ, through the offering of gifts to us.[3]

The challenge for each person is to discern those gifts and accept them by expressing them. That is how Christ sets us free from the captivity to which we have often enslaved ourselves by the choices we make for our own lives.

The perfectionist son ignored the gifts his father would have given him by not asking and not accepting what the father would have gladly imparted. It wasn't the father's fault the perfectionist son never had a party with his friends. We must take responsibility for the recognition and acceptance of our gifts through their expression, and for the resentment that naturally builds with our failure to respond.

But although each of us must take responsibility for our own life, Christ did not intend this to be an isolated endeavor. People were designed by God to need each other. The church is a community where we are called to help each other in this endeavor of discovery. A true community of joy wants all its members to be freed by Christ from their captivity through a recognition of the gifts he has given them. A community of joy also finds ways its members can make that happen, so it becomes the place where people *experience* that freedom and personal joy.

So gifts are designed to be for both the gifted individual and the community of which they are a part. "They are given ... that all may be benefited" (Doctrine and Covenants 46:4).

Vera Entwistle, the founder of Camp Quality (a camping and support program for children with cancer), is gifted in relating to children and in administrative and leadership skills. When she moved to Sydney, Australia, and discovered an unmet need, she mobilized her gifts to organize the first Camp Quality.

In one of her first experiences, she talked to the children in the cancer ward of a hospital. They were alive with excitement at the prospect of a camp they might be able to attend and full of suggestions of what such a camp would need. One boy was particularly enthusiastic. As Vera was about to leave, this boy piped up, "Hey lady! When are you going to have this camp?"

"Well," Vera replied, "I don't know. I've only been in the country a couple of weeks. I don't know anybody. I don't have a campgrounds. I think it wouldn't be till at least next year."

"That's great!" he said. "I hope you can do it, because these kids really need it. But I won't be here by then."

Vera left the hospital determined that there would be a camp for that little boy that summer. Her giftedness and her willingness to employ those gifts enabled the first Camp Quality to happen that summer. And that little boy was there. It was a highlight of his short life.

Because of Vera's gifts, Camp Quality has spread to more than ten countries since that first camp. One boy at the Camp Quality in Kentucky was once asked by a reporter what he liked most about Camp Quality. He replied, "Everybody loves me here." Thousands of children all over the world now experience the love, acceptance, and fun of Camp Quality. They are the recipients of Vera's giftedness.

Yet I have heard Vera say many many times, "If you ask me who benefits the most from Camp Quality, I'll tell you: you're looking at her." "[Gifts] are given ... that all may be benefited."

So what are gifts? They are empowerments through which the presence of the Holy Spirit is extended among humankind. When people are expressing giftedness, the receivers and the giver experience a blessing of the Spirit. This blessing might be manifested in such ways as a powerful sense of God's presence, an awareness of his great love for them, or a heightened understanding of life's mysteries. And this is how a gift differs from a talent.

A talent is an inherent ability to do something well. A person expressing a talent, and the people receiving the benefits of that expression, generally feel a sense of satisfaction, pleasure, and enjoyment. They are entertained. A gift goes beyond that. The expression of giftedness fosters ministry. This ministry can manifest itself in edification for both the gifted individual and the community that receives the gift. A sense of joy, fulfillment, and purpose radiates from the individual and the community. The result is ministry rather than entertainment.

Sometimes God uses a person's talent as a vehicle to express a gift. A gifted speaker, for example, may focus primarily on secular topics. However, there may be times that due to the setting and circumstances, a particular speech is inspired and the power of the Holy Spirit flows in a way that transforms the talent into a gift and brings a blessing to the giver and/or the receivers. For a person who is talented, these occasions of blessing would be isolated. For a person who is gifted, these occasions would happen on a regular basis.

This brings us to an area of giftedness that is often misunderstood. People cannot "turn on" their gifts. People cannot turn talents into gifts at their own will. An important principle of giftedness is that God is the one who bestows gifts.

> Now there are varieties of gifts, but the same Spirit; and there are varieties of services, but the same Lord; and there are varieties of activities, but it is the same God who activates all of them in everyone.—I Corinthians 12:4–6 NRSV

When I was younger, I wanted very much to sing well. I wasn't content to be gifted in other musical areas. I was pretty sure that most people didn't consider me to be much of a soloist. My family teased me when I sang. No one ever gave me positive feedback when I sang for church. But I was determined. I was sure I could manufacture a beautiful voice for myself if I just tried hard enough. So I started voice lessons in high school.

After graduation I went to Graceland as a music major with a vocal emphasis. Every Monday afternoon various students performed at student seminars. I was sure I was improving under the tutelage of my vocal instructor. Then one Monday, the department chairman invited me to his office after the seminar and suggested I choose another area of emphasis. It had taken awhile, but I finally admitted to myself that I was not gifted in singing.

This is not to say that if people do poorly at something initially, they should immediately consider themselves not gifted in that area. A person is well advised to pursue interests and opportunities until it seems fairly well confirmed that he or she either does or does not have a particular gift. We can develop a dormant gift, but we cannot manufacture a gift through our efforts alone.

We must rely on God's grace to inspire our gifts at the right time. And we must be on guard for those who deceive people with their charisma or by manufacturing what appear to be gifts. Jesus said to his disciples: "Beware of false prophets, who come to you in sheep's clothing but inwardly are ravenous wolves. You will know them by their fruits" (Matthew 7:15–16 RSV). We can identify these false prophets by examining and evaluating their fruits.

Paul, in his letter to the Galatians, wrote: "the fruit of the Spirit is love, joy, peace, patience, kindness, goodness, faithfulness, gentleness, self-control" (Galatians 5:22–23 RSV). The gifts of God to humankind will foster these kinds of fruits.

One way we can help to assure that the exercise of giftedness remains authentic and the fruits unblemished is to remember,

> Do not think of yourself more highly than you ought to think, but think with sober judgment, each according to the measure of faith that God has assigned. For . . . we have gifts that differ according to the grace given to us.
>
> —Romans 12:3–6

And,

> You are equal in worth of position and place in the work of the church; and if in honor you shall prefer one another, you will not strive for precedence or a place in duty or privilege, and shall be blessed of me.
>
> —Doctrine and Covenants 122:16b

It seems to be natural that the members of the body consider some to be more important than others. I know people with the wonderful gift of hospitality who look admiringly at a person with the gift of preaching while not even recognizing their own giftedness. The scriptures are clear that all are gifted and that all gifts have equal importance. And all people have equal importance. The giftedness of a person does not determine his or her stature.

If we want our communities to be places where personal giftedness thrives, we must nurture everyone's giftedness, including our own. We can be attentive and observant to the ways we are blessed by the ministry of each person and let them know. Tell people when the exercise of their gifts has blessed you. This important affirmation helps confirm their giftedness and assures that all gifts will be looked on as equally important.

Think how often you express to a gifted preacher the blessing you received. But how often do you tell the greeter who has the gift of hospitality how blessed you were by their ministry? This is one of the reasons we begin to think of the inspired preacher as more important. Unfortunately, because we are human, the disparate show of appreciation for one gift over another also makes it difficult for the person receiving the accolades to remain humble and to "not think of [themselves] more highly than [they] ought."

It is vitally important to give encouraging feedback to people when you have experienced a blessing from the exercise of their gifts. It is also vitally important that the feedback be spread around in equal portions.

Another reason we often experience problems in this area is that we are not intentional enough about asking people to serve in their areas of giftedness. We think of our congregations as having a multitude of jobs to fill. So we ask whoever we think will be willing to take the job, or fulfill the obligation. Or worse yet, we cajole people into filling roles they either don't want to do or don't have the time to do well.

It's hard for me to imagine anyone who hasn't been in this position at one time or another. So the results of this practice probably sound familiar: frustration, resentment, a feeling of failure, and burnout. My experience is that a congregation filled with people who are frustrated, resentful, and burned-out is not a very pleasant place to be and certainly not a place where much ministry is happening. However, if we focus on using people in their areas of giftedness we have a totally different atmosphere. The person expressing the gift feels uplifted and exhilarated.

I know if I had a choice of two church school classes, and one was taught by someone who was unhappy and frustrated because they knew their class was a dud, and one by someone who had the gift of teaching which resulted in a class that was exciting and edifying, I'd go to the latter. Conversely, I'd rather teach an adult class, where I feel excited and energized, than teach a children's class and feel like a failure. If our churches are to be communities of joy they must be filled with people giving ministry, not people doing jobs.

If you are interested in exploring which gifts you have and helping members of your congregation discover their gifts, I suggest you use an excellent resource recently published by Herald House, *Discover and Share Your Gifts*, by Jack Conway, Harry Doty, and Roy Schaefer.[4] I have taught material from this resource in many different settings over the last twelve years, as a field tester and since publication. It always receives an enthusiastic response and people find it helpful and motivating.

As a former pastor, I used these principles in my congregation. My pastoral team made a firm commitment to each other that we would do everything in our power to utilize people only in areas they were gifted. Unfortunately our churches have a deeply ingrained mentality that everyone should get their turn to do everything. Despite our commitment, we often found it difficult to stick to our promise, especially when scheduling preachers.

However, we must believe the wisdom of the following words from the Doctrine and Covenants: "All are called according to the gifts of God to them" (119:8, 156:9). We need to use people to do what they have been called by God to do. That calling is reflected by their giftedness.

Although we committed ourselves to this standard, we still faced the same question I am asked by almost every group where I have taught these principles. What should we do when there are ministries that must be provided (such as a children's church school class) and a truly gifted person is not available? We recognized that we could not transform our congregation overnight to gifts-based ministry. So we did the best we could with what we had.

An amazing thing happened. The areas where we *were* using gifted leaders began to attract more people. Inactive members began attending. People from other congregations transferred their membership. Baptisms increased. Soon our pool of gifted individuals grew, and gradually more and more "jobs" became "ministries."

I watched these principles put into action. I saw them work. I saw people excited about what they were doing and enjoying the ministry of others as their needs were also met. I watched a congregation literally transform before my very eyes into a community of joy. It was the most exciting and rewarding experience of my entire life.

However, I fell into a common trap. I was so enthused I allowed myself to become overcommitted. My life got out of balance. Yes, everything I was doing was good. Yes, I was gifted in all my areas of endeavor. But I forgot the words of Alma: "See that all these things are done in wisdom and order; for it is not requisite that a [person] should run faster than [they] have strength."

Multigifted individuals need to take care that in their enthusiasm they do not take on too much at the same time. If we look to God for guidance, the Spirit will direct us to the areas of giftedness we can best focus on. In time the focus will shift and other gifts will take precedence. But it is vitally important to keep one's life in balance.

In my case, the move I mentioned earlier occurred during my exciting pastoral experience. After the move, I chose to take a break. This was probably wise. Soon I began to fill my life with activity again. But this time my activity excluded rather than encompassed many of my areas of giftedness. By the time I crashed and burned, I really didn't understand what had happened.

So along with the other sources from which I sought guidance, I also looked to my evangelists blessing. In part it states: "As you reach out with ... a greater desire to be expressive in terms of that which is beautiful, and to give your life in creative endeavor in use of talents that you will find that God is very near."

The two creative gifts that have brought me the most joy as I have actively expressed them have been painting and playing the piano. When my mid-life crisis hit, I was involved in lots of activities that utilized other gifts. But I didn't feel God very near. Hence my emptiness. In examining the situation, I realized that I had not painted for six years and had scarcely played the piano for two years. I almost felt guilty about giving them my time because I enjoyed them so much.

I realized that I had allowed overwork in other areas of giftedness to send my life careening out of balance. I am once again finding a sense of fulfillment and purpose in my life as I create time for the gifts God has called me to utilize, and bring them into better balance with the expression of my other gifts. I once again feel God is very near. And as I sense that those gifts are accepted and appreciated by my faith community, I have found joy again. I have found my way home.

My heart reaches out to those in our congregations who are struggling in the mire of personal emptiness, as I was. Let us help these people discover their gifts. Let us appreciate who they are through the acceptance of their gifts. Let us find avenues that allow them to express that giftedness in ways that will bless both them and the body. Because to the degree that we are able to realize this in our congregations, they will become communities of joy for the people who call those congregations "home."

Each chapter that follows focuses on a single area of giftedness and discusses it in depth. They certainly do not exhaust the list of God-given gifts but encompass a significant variety of ministries that take place in a joyful community. May we always be found working together to find which gifts reside in ourselves and each other. May we always be found utilizing people with those gifts in their areas of giftedness. Then will the people rise up and say, "In our community of Christ, we count it all joy!"

Study Questions

1. Think about times you have felt aimless and without direction. Write down what was happening in your life at that time and how you felt. Are there two or three who care to share their experience with the class?
2. Write down what you consider to be one to three of your most significant gifts. How did you feel when you were expressing those gifts? How did you feel when you were not expressing those gifts? Would two or three share?
3. What is the difference between the prodigal son and the perfectionist son? How many identify with the prodigal son? Would anyone care to share your experience and what caused you to desire a change in your life? Who identifies with the perfectionist son? Would any of you like to share your experience? Have you come to the point that you want a change in your life?
4. Read Psalm 68:18 aloud. Read Ephesians 4:8 aloud. How does the writer of Ephesians change the quotation from the Book of Psalms? What does this change mean?

5. What is the difference between a talent and a gift? What are the results of the expression of talents? What are the results of the expression of gifts? Give examples of a person who expressed a talent and another person who expressed the same thing as a gift. For example, the ability to speak well was expressed by Adolph Hitler as a talent, by Peter Marshall as a gift.
6. What is our role in discovering and developing our gifts? What is God's role?
7. How can we tell if a gift is authentic or counterfeit?
8. How can we help confirm people's giftedness? How can our own giftedness be confirmed?
9. What does gifts-based ministry mean? Do you think this is a goal for which we should strive? Why or why not?
10. What does the word "requisite" mean? What happens to the gifted individual who tries to express too many areas of giftedness at the same time? What can happen to other members of the congregation? What can happen to the congregation?

Notes

1. Kent Ira Groff, *Active Spirituality: A Guide for Seekers and Ministers* (New York: The Alban Institute, 1993), 18–20.
2. Ibid., 20.
3. William Barclay, *The Daily Study Bible: The Letters to the Galatians and Ephesians.* (Philadelphia: Westminster Press, 1975), 143.
4. John T. Conway, Harry L. Doty, and Roy H. Schaefer, *Discover and Share Your Gifts* (Independence, Missouri: Herald Publishing House, 1994).

2

Uplifting Congregational Worship

Kenneth L. McLaughlin

I have experienced uplifting congregational worship many times in my life. Some of these experiences have been in spectacular outdoor settings; others amidst the majestic harmonies of timeless, classical music. They have been led by highly skilled and sensitive presiders, planned by women and men amazingly able to weave together disparate elements into a unified tapestry of praise, and facilitated by a variety of participants representing all ages and life perspectives. These worship experiences–within and those outside the RLDS tradition–have been blessed by articulate, trained, and theologically mature preachers.

But I have also been in uplifting congregational worship in poorly planned and aesthetically unpleasant buildings, and amidst musical numbers blaring from inexpensive "boom boxes" operated by not-so-electronically gifted people. These uplifting events have been presided over by relatively unskilled and insensitive people, planned in haphazard and (most likely) last-minute fashion, and shared in by nondiverse worship facilitators who did not reflect the makeup of the congregation. Often, the preachers at these events have ranged from ill-trained to theologically shallow.

I have also experienced uplifting congregational worship in a host of circumstances that fall between these two extremes.

Uplifting worship, at least as I understand it, simply cannot be characterized, classified, and generalized by location, component, competency, or style. The uplifting nature of worship goes beyond musical selection, dress code, variety, and duration.

But *don't get me wrong*. I firmly believe that worship can be greatly enhanced by factors such as good planning, competent leadership, a lovely setting, and effective artistic expression. Such things, in fact, greatly increase the likelihood of uplifting worship. Yet somehow, in a way that is both mysterious and awesome, uplifting worship transcends the human ability to prescribe, describe, summarize, and easily replicate.

This chapter *is* about uplifting congregational worship, but it is *not* about worship planning, liturgics, skills development, or procedure. It does not contain "ten steps to uplifting worship." Instead, I have chosen to identify some common qualities that appear to me to be a part of the many expressions of uplifting worship in which I have participated.

These five commonalities include: (1) relevancy to the human condition; (2) response to the yearning to connect; (3) concrete articulation of the faith; (4) emotive and artistic expression of human feelings; and (5) recognition of God's immanence, transcendence, and absence.

Relevancy to the Human Condition

I remember standing in the foyer of the church where my mother attends. Norma, a good friend for many years, greeted me after I delivered the morning sermon. "Kenny," she said (and only my dear and long-standing friends would greet me with my childhood nickname), "how is it that every time you preach here it seems that you're speaking directly to me and what is on my mind?" I assured Norma I was no mind reader, but that I tried very hard to make sure my remarks clearly and directly spoke to human conditions, including the problems all of us face. "Norma, I wasn't speaking to you any more than I was talking to myself. Even though there are vast differences among all people, we are still more alike than different."

Last year, when I began ministering in the Pan-Pacific Field of the church as a member of the Council of Twelve, I worried that I would have little to say that would be helpful to the people who lived in nations far from my own and in cultures vastly different from the only culture I knew. My fears were soon diminished when I realized that the center of human life transcends national boundaries, languages, and lifestyles. As I participated in worship with the assistance of able translators, I could sense being connected by heart and mind to God's international family of love.

The human condition includes the full range of thought and emotion. It involves experiences of intense joy and sorrow, victory and defeat, excitement and boredom, courage and fear, hope and despair, and everything in between. Too often we try to worship as if life didn't offer all these expressions. We fail to realize that authentic worship does not ignore unpleasantries or hide behind what is superficial and artificial. Rather, it celebrates all of life and acknowledges both the good and the tragic.

Uplifting worship may cause us to explore the mysteries of the universe, but it never ignores or fails to celebrate the simple, wonderful gift of life given one day at a time and filled with risks and uncertain direction.

If worship is to be uplifting, it must include elements that address the specific, current circumstances of the worshipers, the church neighborhood, and the world community. I can recall vividly worship experiences that truly welcomed newborn babies, gave voice to battered women, allowed men to confess their difficulty with feeling deeply, or welcomed back at worship with open arms the returning college student or the elderly who had faced difficult surgery. I can still hear the words of sensitive ministers speaking about civil unrest, world hunger, and racial tension. I continue to find joy in remembering powerful moments of reconciliation, statements of personal victory over addictions or toxic behavior, and the simple lessons of children teaching adults the timeless message of the birth of Jesus and about divine love for the world.

I still give silent thanks each time I recall a youth camp worship where young people came to the awesome reality that God loved them and would be with them each moment of life. Uplifting worship is a continuous recognition and celebration of our humanity.

Response to the Yearning to Connect

Twenty-five years ago, while a freshman at Ohio State University, I lived through the trauma of the campus riots and war protests that resulted in the deaths of four people at another Ohio school, Kent State. I recall being tear-gassed by National Guard troops while leaving my political science class one warm and tense May morning. Through burning eyes, I remember looking out on a world that had gone crazy, where political and social ignorance led to devastating results.

After the campus closed and the students were ordered out of their dormitories, I recall driving home and looking forward to being at church that Wednesday night to mourn with my congregational family and to pray for the restoration of sanity both at home and in Vietnam. I remember wanting to connect with my church family and with God in an environment of trust and support, where my sadness could be expressed in a loving community of friends and believers.

Despite North American culture's strong focus on individual achievement and private freedom to act, I believe human beings are primarily social creatures who yearn to live–and need to live–in community. We are created by an ever-gracious God who seeks to be present in all of life's activities. The central reason for human failure is alienation and separation from self, others, and God. Abundant life, on the other hand, stems from the healthy relationship between self with self, self with others, and self with God and God's vast and marvelous creation.

Uplifting worship satisfies this need to connect. It provides opportunity to speak words of praise, to touch other living flesh, and to stand in awe at the beauty of the planet. It allows us to embrace the unspeakable desire to belong and be part of something greater than our own isolated selves.

The various elements of uplifting worship must take advantage of all the senses and give opportunity for worshipers to examine and reflect on those parts of life that are imbalanced, out of focus, and fragmented. There should be time for confession and resolve, for dialogue, and for silence. Uplifting worship is rooted in the affirmation that God's intention is that life should be lived together–all together–in communities of joy, hope, love, and peace.

Our faith movement is rooted in a community-building tradition. While the specific ideas of our forebears about community building may seem rather naive and quaint to us now, the underlying principles found in the early years of the Restoration are as viable and powerful today as 165 years ago. God's intention is for all creation to be connected, not only by virtue of divine design, but also by our recognition and celebration of that connectedness. Uplifting worship always provides opportunities for our alienated beings to be restored in healthy and life-promoting community.

Concrete Articulation of the Faith

One Sunday morning I recall leaving the sanctuary of my home congregation after a worship service that left me feeling rather empty, almost depressed. I couldn't put my finger on what was troubling me. The service was fairly cohesive, with a variety of elements and participants. The theme of the day and the remarks that were made were neither depressing nor negative. As I stood outside talking to one of my friends, we began to analyze the morning worship. It didn't take long for us to figure out the problem. No one had bothered to clearly state that this was a Christian gathering, anchored in the "Good News" of the life, teaching, death, and resurrection of Jesus Christ. No one called us together as disciples, or read from the sacred texts of scripture. The preacher failed to link his remarks to the declaration of the gospel. No one communicated the foundational Christian messages of hope, reconciliation, compassion, justice, transformation, or new life. The worship experience could have just as easily been a meeting of a secular social or service club.

Uplifting worship involves the intentional proclamation of Jesus Christ. This is far more than simply stating the name of Jesus or using flowery or trite expressions that have a Christian flavor to them. Christian proclamation is a "living out" of the model provided for us by our Savior. It involves blending our words and deeds in a way that says clearly to those around us, and to ourselves, that we are followers of Jesus Christ. It says that we have elected to anchor our lives and expend our energies in the service of the One who gave us a vision of God's global community of peace and justice which we call Zion.

Proclamation should be neither subtle nor anemic. It cannot be diluted to be made palatable to a culture that is becoming increasingly secular. Proclamation, whether spoken in hushed tones or shouted exuberantly, never leaves the listener in doubt about the motives and mission of the proclaimer.

Proclamation is more than the mindless recitation of Christian clichés and pleasantries. Too often worship is prevented from soaring because worship leaders fail to find fresh and meaningful ways to clearly articulate the faith message. Moreover, leaders often deal with peripheral issues of the faith or are distracted by matters that have precious little to do with offering new and abundant life to those who take upon them the name and cause of Christ.

It takes courage and insight to interpret the gospel message contextually, in ways that make sense to children, women, and men of this time and this place. A clear, concrete proclamation of the Christian message can assist people to hear the old, old story in new, alive, and relevant images.

Uplifting worship reinforces the core values of Christianity. It does not shrink from the task of calling people to forgiveness and reconciliation. It teaches lessons of honesty and integrity, of courage and selflessness. Uplifting worship affirms the value of compassionate love and mutuality. It speaks of equal regard for others and unconditional acceptance. It gives room for exploring new ways to incorporate ageless values into contemporary lifestyles. Uplifting worship issues challenges and calls people to envision a world where mercy and justice are found in every heart and in every societal and political institution.

Emotive and Artistic Expression of Human Feelings

Last Sunday I sat in a congregation and was greatly blessed by the worship experience. The presider, a woman in her early twenties, encouraged the congregation to engage in the celebration of children and to experience the same joy Jesus must have experienced as he called the little ones to his side, where they were blessed. The service included dance, voice choir, a clearly stated message of the pricelessness of children, as well as a beautiful new hymn. Those leading the worship experience included some people not often asked to be "up front." The service spoke of the universal desire for peace and the difference one person can make. Many of the worship elements evoked an emotional response, and there was artistic expression, all amateur but sincerely and conscientiously executed throughout. I left thinking how happy I was to have been present.

I cannot think of one single uplifting congregational worship experience that did not involve some kind of artistic expression and emotive response. We humans have a need to express many of our deepest thoughts and aspirations in artistic ways. A single beautiful song, an inspiring painting, or the power of poetically arranged words all call forth responses from us that are difficult to describe. They are the stuff of which deep and lasting beauty is made.

A few years ago I attended a Christian worship service in what is often referred to as a "megachurch." The pastor's theology was clearly evangelical, and his message contained virtually no content with which I agreed. This was especially true of those portions dealing with family roles and women's issues. But I must confess that in the midst of such a setting, there were musical and testimonial offerings that moved me deeply because of the emotional power of the delivery and the opportunity it gave me to connect with my feelings. Also, as I sat in the congregation, there was a certain group energy that drew me in. People were intentionally engaged in praise and thanksgiving. They openly greeted one another with handshakes and hugs. Most were quick to respond to the chance to pray for those seated around them.

It is no secret that within the RLDS tradition there are strongly held opinions concerning what is appropriate and inappropriate in worship, particularly regarding forms of artistic expression. Often we pride ourselves on our tolerance of diversity in worship expression. But it is my observation that the closer we are to our own congregation, the less tolerance we have for innovations in worship practices.

I have witnessed otherwise open-minded people become outraged at the thought of uplifted hands during worship. Others have become upset at the inclusion of country music, or plastic flowers, or dance, or young people in shorts and tank tops, or anything that involves getting up and moving around the room, or using taped praise music, or . . . you get the point.

It is difficult for me to believe that God cares a great deal about things like whether we use taped music or plastic flowers or go to church in shorts. I no longer can fathom that God cares about the elements we choose for worship so much as God cares about the fact that we intentionally come together *for* worship with sincerity of purpose and intent, offering our best gifts to honor the Divine and to bless the gathered community.

Some seem displeased when those in the worship service are not particularly polished at what they contribute. Here I am not referring to displeasure caused by a participant's lack of preparation or interest in improving the quality of public ministry. I am also not talking about those whose theological perspectives are unhealthy to the congregation. Rather, I am talking about those who are trying to do their best, but simply are not particularly gifted. Somehow we must seek to eliminate mediocrity in worship and yet celebrate and bless the contribution that each one is able to bring. It is no easy task.

It is time, within our movement, to widen our spectrum of acceptability when it comes to the inclusion of emotive and artistic elements in worship. Perhaps it is time to acknowledge that in many congregations our worship speaks too much to the head and not enough to the heart. Perhaps it is time for our worship experiences to be filled with unrestrained laughter, applause, unashamed tears, shouting, toe-tapping, silence, embracing, dancing, and more. Perhaps it is time for a new celebration of feeling without abandoning the intellect.

Recognition of God's Immanence, Transcendence, and Absence

Several months ago I sat in a modest church facility in Suva, the capital city of the Fiji Islands. The room was packed with worshipers of all ages and of several cultural and ethnic backgrounds. The participants spoke in three different languages, yet were united in their desire to be together and in the universal quality of the sacraments that were celebrated that morning. The singing was enthusiastic, and there was a genuine sense of joy. In those moments I felt God right there with us in a power and presence that filled up my being and was undeniable throughout that wonderful morning.

A few years ago I shared with a congregation as its worship explored the creative genius of God seen in the vastness and complexity of the universe. I recall a dark blue banner hanging in front of the church. At its center was a photograph of the earth taken from one of the Apollo spacecrafts. The preacher used as his scriptural text one of the Genesis accounts of creation. He emphasized the goodness of creation as well as the Creator. The service caused me to reflect on the enormity of God "out there" pervading all of time and space. I took comfort in sharing in the affirmation that all of this wonderful planet and everything beyond belong to God.

While living in Ohio I participated in the planning and execution of a worship service that emphasized those times in life when we experience the desert: symbolic of struggle, loneliness, and doubt. The service was sober and contemplative, and it caused the congregation to remain quiet, without animation. The service called into question the presence of God at times when all that is felt is absence. Even so, the service was uplifting in its recognition of the potential for growth, focus, and new connections to God that are found in taking advantage of time spent in the desert.

The three experiences I have just described all speak to the recognition of God in life and in worship. The first affirmed those wonderful moments when we can declare that God is close at hand, or immanent. Often these are the experiences we most long for. They bring us a joy and reassurance that is vital for a healthy life in the faith. They reconfirm our desire to be able to share intimacy with the Divine.

The second experience described the transcedence of God. Here the congregation had opportunity to focus on the reality of God that goes beyond our limited framework of time, space, and location. Such worship keeps us in balance and gives perspective as we marvel at the vastness of God's domain.

The third allowed the community of the faithful to explore those times when, despite our best desires, all we feel is God's absence. Such worship experiences provide the congregation with an honest environment in which to seek God and declare our deepest desires for connection in the midst of an often hostile and uncaring world.

Too often worship is entered into without much thought about the opportunity of "God-encounter." We simply forget to take even a few moments to focus on what worship is all about and what can occur. Even presiding ministers, in their opening greetings, have the opportunity to restate the purpose for gathering and the potential present for a satisfying and life-enhancing experience together.

Worship entered into without much thought, purpose, or expectation is likely to have little impact on the gathered community. The intentional recognition of God in our midst greatly increases the opportunity for meaningful worship.

Conclusion

Worship is central to the life of the Christian community. It speaks to the very heart and soul of the church, and provides opportunity for the sweet celebration of life. I cannot fathom a way to "count it all joy" without meeting regularly with my sisters and brothers of the faith in uplifting moments where we connect with one another and with the Creator. These moments are ever ripe with the potential for experiencing the gospel in ways relevant to our time and place, bringing honor to God and giving purpose to our being.

Study Questions

1. Do you agree with the author's observation that uplifting worship "simply cannot be characterized or classified or generalized by location component, competency, or style?" If so, then why spend so much time and effort in worship planning?
2. The author discusses five common qualities that are present in uplifting worship. Would you add any other commonalities or disagree with any of the ones he has listed?
3. Do your congregational worship services specifically talk about the "human condition"? In what ways? Would your young adults and youth agree that your worship is relevant to today's world? What subjects are avoided in your congregational worship?
4. What worship elements or techniques are available to a congregation that truly wishes to have its members feel connected to one another? Is the worship service the best time to build a sense of community?
5. The author believes that uplifting worship must intentionally proclaim Jesus. What does the author mean by proclamation? What are some ways to specifically articulate the Christian faith during worship?
6. The author states, "It is difficult for me to believe that God cares a great deal about things like whether we use taped music or plastic flowers or go to church in shorts." Should this be taken as advocating that "anything goes"? What is the author trying to say about our personal opinions concerning what is appropriate for worship?
7. What do the terms "immanence" and "transcendence" mean in relationship to God? How do you personally most often experience God? Should there be a place in worship to acknowledge that at times what we feel most is God's absence?

3

Positive Preaching

Danny A. Belrose

The sermon was dragging on–longer and longer. The preacher was droning on–duller and duller. From a far corner of the church came the clear, plaintive question of a five year old: "Mommy, can we please just pay the man and go home?"[1]

Preaching should be a joyful, positive experience for the listeners and for the speaker. My first sermon was neither. Hours of blood, sweat, and tears had produced a two-page single-spaced typed manuscript. I was pleased with the profound thoughts that had poured themselves (with considerable coaxing) onto those inspired pages. I approached the appointed hour with a mixture of excitement and anxiety. I thought, "This is going to be good! This is going to be life-changing! Souls will be brought to Jesus. This will be memorable!" And it was.

Sunday morning came. The final chords of a congregational hymn reverberated around the sanctuary. I stood and moved toward the pulpit. The five feet separating me from the *sacred desk* suddenly became the length of a bowling alley. I seemed out of breath. I laid the pages of my manuscript side-by-side like two stone tablets. My eyes zoomed in on the large schoolroom clock which hung like a brooding silent sentinel over the entrance to the small sanctuary. I was no stranger to the *big* clock. It had been nemesis to preacher and parishioner alike. As a child I had marveled that the *big* clock could run like a racehorse, completely stand still, and yes, even go backwards. It all depended on who was preaching.

I smiled. *Big* clock smiled back. "Eleven twenty a.m. and all is well!" it shouted to me, "You have all the time you need. I am your friend!" I launched into my clever introduction. Every eye was riveted on me. Hearts and minds were open. Crying infants were struck dumb. I proceeded methodically point by point until I had completed my prepared manuscript. I gazed at the *big* clock. It whispered, "Eleven twenty-six a.m. and all is well. You have all the time you need. I am your friend." I panicked. My mind whirled. Six minutes? Six minutes and I'm finished? No way! Couldn't be! I had just shared *everything* I knew about the gospel and it was eleven twenty-six. What to do? I could start again ... maybe I should repeat the ending for emphasis! *Big* clock frowned. I sat down. *Big* clock grinned. "Eleven twenty-seven and all is well. You have all the time you need. When you have nothing to say, remember to sit down. I am your friend."

Subsequent preaching opportunities found me absorbed with expanding my sermon material in an almost desperate attempt to "occupy the hour." Time took on more importance than the sermon. I had not listened to the clock. "You have all the time you need. I am your friend." It was a long time before I came to the realization that sermons do not *fill* time; they *shape* time! Positive sermons shape time and can be used by the Holy Spirit to shape and reshape the life of preacher and listener. But good sermons must themselves be shaped. They must be wisely constructed and carry the music of God's Spirit.

Without the Spirit the Music Is Dead

Both the wise and foolish builder in Jesus' parable expended considerable energy in constructing their respective houses. We assume that the foolish builder was lazy and took the easy way out. But building a house on sand may require more work than building one on rock. Shifting and eroding sand could cause delays and duplicated efforts to shore things up. There were probably design modifications, additional expenses, and more time required to offset unseen problems. This builder was not foolish because he built his house on sand; he was foolish because he *continued to build* on sand. Some preachers are like this. They continue to do what they have always done and wonder why their sermons are miracle cures for insomnia! The foolish builder failed to learn what the sand was telling him: "Don't build on me; I can't be depended on!"

Positive preachers do not depend on this month's *Reader's Digest* the Saturday night before Sunday's sermon. Good preachers must have "something important to say," they must "want desperately to say it," and they must "say it well!" It is not enough, however, to simply have something important to say. The focus of the message must be centered in the good news and hope of the gospel; otherwise, it will *not* be a sermon! The purpose of preaching is to be a vehicle for the Holy Spirit.

Wise preachers know what to depend on. The secret of good preaching is spiritual renewal and refreshment. Sermons will not stand if they are not shaped by the Holy Spirit. One cannot speak of the God one does not know. Effective preachers not only immerse themselves in disciplined study habits and prayer, but continually discover the presence of the Divine in all of life's relationships. Whether one is reading a mystery novel, watching a movie, sitting on a park bench, or having a quiet conversation with friends, God is never absent.

Spiritual refreshment comes from participating in the lives of people. People are the primary liturgical documents. Illustrations and themes crowd you when you share in the lives of others. Thomas H. Troeger says,

> Preaching depends on the Spirit. . . . You may have perfected every method and technique, but without the Spirit the music is dead. . . . Follow the pull of the Spirit to return to the Source, to God who made you and Christ who redeemed you. Understand all of your imaginative work as an effort to return to the Source.[2]

Does this mean one simply increases one's piety? Crank up the fasting and prayer and let the Holy Spirit take over? Some speakers don't do any shaping. They just let it happen. They proceed to the pulpit and expect God to preach the sermon. To them advanced preparation is a lack of faith. They function as if the Holy Spirit only inspires preachers between eleven a.m. and noon Sunday.

Occasionally one may be called on to occupy the pulpit having no specific advanced warning or preparation. But, as a rule, when people preach without preparation, they shortchange the congregation and insult God. David Schlafer, author of *Surviving the Sermon: A Guide to Preaching*, writes,

> God has promised that the divine word will not return empty—in spite of, if not because of the preacher. The church believes that the sacraments are valid regardless of the moral worth of the minister. This does not mean that tales told by idiots are, by divine transmutation, rendered the songs of angels.[3]

The Sacrament of the Word

What is it we are shaping? What is a sermon? What is preaching? Is it a talk?—a lecture?—a means to educate? Philips Brooks refers to preaching as "the sharing of truth through personality." Preaching is ultimately a sacred conversation. It is an experience wherein both preacher and listener encounter what Donald Coggin refers to as "the sacrament of the Word." Coggin, retired archbishop of Canterbury says, "effective preaching is not merely a series of words or reports; instead, it is intended by God as an actual creative extension of the Word of Life."[4] A presentation may be well crafted, theologically sound, masterfully delivered and entertaining, but if it does not clearly proclaim the redeeming grace of the gospel it will not be a sermon!

For some, preaching is not a sacred act but simply an elongated lesson that dominates a worship service. We have become so adept at dividing the sacred from the secular that we divide the sacred from the *not-as-sacred*. All sacraments are symbolic in nature and are a means of divine communication. The symbols of water, bread, wine, consecrated oil, and laying on of hands serve to "say something" that cannot be said in any other way. They are ordinary things made extraordinary. They become redemptive agents blessed beyond their "everyday" capacity. We encounter and appropriate the redeeming presence of the Divine by participating in the messages they convey. I suggest that the divine encounter made possible by preaching (the sacrament of the Word) is no less valid than the rites we traditionally refer to as sacramental. The redeeming power of the Holy Spirit actualized through aural symbolism renders the act of preaching a sacred conversation. In Thomas Troeger's words,

> In a sense, the voice of the preacher is an aural symbol, just as the chalice, the altar, and the cross are visual symbols. Paul Tillich has said that they draw us beyond what they are in themselves toward the ultimate reality that is their source, and this is precisely what good sermons do. The preacher's voice uses words and the physical properties of sound to draw people beyond the message that is being articulated into the presence of God.[5]

Preaching must redeem us from our worst enemies: unbelief, self-absorption, futility, anxiety, fear, anger, and lust; and equip us with trust, purpose, serenity, joy, hope, love, and peace. Such redemption *is* sacramental. Perhaps we have failed to appropriate preaching in a sacramental sense because we tend to think of preaching as a monologue–a one-way communication.

No Monologues Please: First Things First!

Positive preaching is not a monologue. We need to put "first things first." Good preaching is response! It begins with *listening*. It is not the voice of one person speaking *for* one person. Rather it is a response to and an expression of many voices beyond the particular voice of the preacher.

I have already indicated that the primary task of the preacher is to be directed by the Holy Spirit. The preacher must discern the Spirit with a listening ear and eye. Sermon preparation should begin by listening to the scripture text suggested by the assigned theme. This means reading the text aloud in your own hearing. It may be helpful to do so in as many translations as possible. Reading the chapter that precedes and follows the given text may help clarify context. When reading the text aloud, listen to the many voices speaking through the text. What is being said here? What is not being said? What am I hearing that I have not heard before? Are there verses, phrases, or words that claim my attention?

Certainly the voices uncovered by biblical criticism, commentaries, and theological reference materials should be heard. Scholarly works are helpful and important tools. But this first hearing of the text should be free from the voices of experts who may compete for the preacher's attention with answers to questions he or she has yet to ask. First things first. Let the text speak for itself.

After reading several versions of the text aloud, examine it again for deeper insights. The following may assist your hearing of the voices within the text:

1. Acknowledge your present attitude. Begin by examining your attitude about authoritative scripture. What bias do you bring to the experience of engaging the text? What claim does scripture have on you? Do you ascribe to plenary revelation? Is it historical fiction, fact, or both? Is it a living witness or a passive record? What familiarity do you bring to it? Are you examining it, or is it examining you? Acknowledge your present attitude to scripture and permit an open verdict. In your exploration, be willing to be surprised.

*2. **Appreciate the scripture's richness.*** Scripture has stood the test of time and continues to inform the faith of millions. Appreciate its unquestioning value.

*3. **Engage the Word before the words.*** Pray for enlightenment as you read. Pray, not merely as a prelude to reading the text, but as a continuous process in engaging the text.

*4. **Overview the selected text.*** Scan the specific text or book. Become familiar with the flow and movement in the writing style. Is it a narrative model? Is there dialogue and action that lends itself to vicarious interplay between the text and the reader?

*5. **Begin at the beginning.*** Does the text have a title? An introduction that hints at its basic message or intent? Does the text suggest whom the writer is addressing and why?

*6. **Examine the ending.*** Is there a summary statement? What is the nature of the conclusion, if any?

*7. **Read what is there–not what is not there.*** "Familiarity breeds contempt." Do not skip over well-known passages. They may surprise and enrich you. Do not ignore uncomfortable material. Do not be quick to sanitize the text because it does not fit your personal theology or viewpoint.

*8. **Let the scripture choose you.*** Let the text speak to you. Contemplate and meditate on verses that appear to stand out or to draw your interest.

*9. **Try to discern the literal meaning.*** Is the text speaking metaphorically, poetically, historically, literally?

*10. **Try to understand the context.*** What is being said to whom, where, and why? What is the life situation? Explore available resources to identify background and setting. Clarify unusual terms, as well as cultural and historical settings. Why is this particular text placed in this location?

*11. **What is being said to you today in your reality?*** What is being said to us today? Is there a message that speaks to contemporary challenges, concerns, and questions?

Preachers must also listen to the voices of the congregation. They must hear and observe the concerns, questions, hurts, sorrows, joys, defeats, and victories of the community of Christ. Sermons that are not responsive *to* and in connection *with* the realities of life do not connect. They are impoverished and unauthentic if they do not powerfully speak *from* as well as *to* and *with* the hearers. Sermons that are not products of community and mutuality are divorced from life and the Spirit. In other words, preaching must be personal! It must be person oriented. At one time I would have said that the sermon must be about *them*; it must be vital to *them*! I have learned that the sermon should be about *us* (the voice of preacher and listener). David Schlafer says,

> The sermon is not a monologue, but an unfolding conversation of the people of God—a conversation about and with God, and about their struggles to know and be faithful to God.[6]

The preacher then is not a theological expert who unfolds the mysteries of God but is a fellow seeker and traveler who shares in the process of discovery with the listeners. This does not mean that he or she abrogates scholarly treatment of the theme or text under consideration. The disciplines and fruits of study can bring needed light to contextual understanding but should never do so at the expense of that to which they point.

In his famous sermon, "The Candle of Lord," Phillips Brooks declared,

> . . . the secret of all pious bigotry, of all holy prejudice is the candle putting its own color into the flame which is borrowed from the fire of God. The violent person makes God seem violent. The feeble person makes God seem feeble. The speculative person makes God look like a beautiful dream. The legal person makes God look like a hard and steel-like jaw.[7]

Positive preachers stand, then, as "candles of the Lord" whose light is enhanced by many voices. They must reflect that light without unduly bending it by their personal bias and prejudice. The sermon must provide the framework for a divine encounter with preacher and listener. Although the sermon may inform and educate, this is *not* its major objective. The pulpit is not a place to do theology. It is a place to offer an invitation! J. Randall Nichols says,

> To preach the gospel, then, is not merely to say words but to effect a deed. To preach is not merely to stand in a pulpit and speak, no matter how eloquently and effectively, not even to set forth a theology, no matter how clearly it is stated nor how worthy the theology. To preach is to become a part of a dynamic event wherein the living, redeeming God reproduces his act of redemption in a living encounter with men through the preacher.[8]

Getting It Across?

Is the invitation being heard? I am constantly amazed when I hear a preacher ask, "How do you know if they are listening? How can you be sure you are getting it across?" My response to the first question is, "Look at the congregation!" If people are looking out the window or adding up yesterday's grocery receipt, they are not listening. If you hear snoring sounds, someone is not listening. If adults borrow crayons from their children so that *they* can color, they are not listening. In short, if you do not have meaningful eye contact and active facial response, they are not listening–and *you* are not listening! Listening does not end with the research and preparation of the sermon. You must listen *as* you preach. Preaching is not a one-way communication. It is communal. It is a dance. The positive preacher listens to the messages transmitted by the congregation. The message may be "We're bored," or "I disagree with that point," or "I don't understand what that means, can you say it in some other way," or "Yes! That's it! That is what I am looking for."

My response to the second question is, "Stop trying to get it across!" Getting it across is not the objective. Eugene Lowry, professor of homiletics at Saint Paul School of Theology, cautions:

> The sermonic goal often becomes narrowed to an educational aim: to inform, to clarify, to apply. And then we measure our success in terms of having "gotten it across"–a very telling phrase.[9]

A sermon, then, should be more descriptive than prescriptive. It should serve to open things up as opposed to lay things out! The authority of the speaker is subsidiary to the authority of the revelatory process between the listener and the Spirit. In other words, truth determines its own value: "All truth is independent in that sphere in which God has placed it, to act for itself" (Doctrine and Covenants 90:5b).

Certainly preachers are challenged to articulate as clearly as possible God's redemptive power, but such power is not exclusively resident within the speaker who must "get it across." It is resident in the preaching experience itself in which the speaker is actively participating as both recipient and spokesperson. The preacher and listener stand on equal ground in the divine encounter engendered through the spoken word. Lowry would say the preacher is seen more as *seeker for* and less an *explainer of* the text ir attempt to make manifest the Word.

How does the Word become manifest in us? It is mani we become a "pavior." Pavior is a fine old English word presses our witness accurately. A pavior was one who paved oad, who prepared the way and made paths straight. John the Baptist was a pavior. The world desperately needs a savior. It also needs paviors.

Positive preachers prepare the way for Christ when they give him leverage in their lives. A receptive mind is an indispensable road-making tool. We prepare the way when we become a crying voice. In the beginning is the word–always! We make paths straight when we bring God's creative word to a world dying for lack of it. We go before God's face and make ready for the unction of the Holy Spirit when we help remove things that block God's entrance into our world: ancestral blindness, sanctified stupidities, sexism, ageism, greed, pride, hatred–sin in its myriad of blatant expressions and disguises.

Positive preachers not only clear the path, they help shape it. Some sermons don't really go anywhere, and the congregation is painfully aware there is no destination or end in sight. They are willing to go at least part way with you when they sense you know where you are going. The question is: Are you on a journey or are you just wandering?

Following the Yellow Brick Road

In *Alice in Wonderland,* Alice asked the cat, "Would you tell me, please, which way I ought to go from here?" The cat replied, "That depends a good deal on where you want to get to." "I don't much care where," said Alice. To which the cat responded, "Then it doesn't matter which way you go." "... so long as I get *somewhere,*" Alice added as an explanation. The cat answered with wisdom and insight, "Oh, you're sure to do that if you only walk long enough."

Dorothy, in *The Wizard of Oz,* willingly followed the yellow brick road because it led to the Emerald City and the Wizard, whom she believed could help her get home. Both Alice and Dorothy were on their way somewhere. But Alice was wandering and Dorothy was on a journey. She desperately wanted to get home; she had a mission and a definite goal in sight. Sermons should have a destination—an aim and a focus. Lowry writes,

> I am convinced that when a text is explored thoroughly, with the preacher asking, "What is the focus here?" rather than " What is the message here?" the homiletical work is energized remarkably. Moreover, the question of focus naturally evokes the question about the turn: "How can this issue get resolved, and where is resolution found?"[11]

All effective sermons have plots, that is, they are mapped out with a focus and aim in mind. Lowry's use of the term "turn" refers to the pivotal turning point of the sermon which brings resolution to a problem or ambiguity around which a sermon may be plotted. But before we get too far down the yellow brick road of sermon plotting, we should look again at how the sermon will be shaped. Sermons are shaped either as narratives, arguments, or images. We will look first at the narrative sermon.

Head High and Heart Deep

Positive preachers know their preaching context. If a sermon is to address the hurts and hopes of the hearers, the preacher has to speak the listener's language. This includes a sensitivity to the theological, educational, and cultural[12] mix of the congregation. Some listeners are analytical and thrive on new ideas and concepts. They want a sermon that is "heady" and mentally stimulating. If it isn't "head high," it isn't a sermon! On the other hand, there are those who couldn't care less about new information; they want to *feel* something. They don't want highfalutin' language. They want to be touched by the sermon; it must be heart deep!

It is a grave mistake to stratify these categories into the learned and unlearned or, for that matter, the unemotional and emotional. Head-high people have feelings and heart-deep people have brains! I am simply talking about different strokes for different folks! The effective sermon will contain both stimulating content and passion. Even the most cerebral sermon should be heart deep. George Herbert, seventeenth-century preacher, admonished preachers about

> dipping and seasoning all our words and sentences in our hearts before they come into our mouths . . . so that the auditors may plainly perceive that every word is "heart-deep."[13]

An understanding of the cultural and congregational context can go a long way in guiding the preacher as to the weight he or she gives to these elements.

Similarly, the preacher needs to be aware of the theological climate of the congregation. Does the congregation have a conservative or liberal bent? And how does that shape the message? The mission of the preacher is not to impose personal theology on the congregation. Preachers must be sensitive to the collective voices of the congregation merged with their own in bringing about an encounter with the Divine. The preacher's task is to proclaim Christ, not to define Divinity. At our very best, we only approximate God.

Does this mean preachers must subvert their own convictions and not give vent to personal faith or theological ideas? Not at all. But the speaker must be cognizant that a sanctuary is not a church school classroom. What is at issue is integrity—the integrity of the preacher and the integrity of the congregation. The key word here is "impose." Neither speaker nor congregation should impose on the other. Yes, new ideas, even ideas that will disturb and stretch viewpoints are at home in the pulpit. Jesus frequently upset his hearers, yet they always gave him voice. They gave him voice because he knew his audience and he spoke their language. People will not give us a hearing if we cannot, first, hear them.

Finally the head-high and heart-deep preachers must have a keen awareness of the potential (if not actual) issues that confront their hearers. Positive preaching does not avoid the unevenness of life. Joy is not the absence of pain but the presence of Christ. Our sermons need to speak to the issues addressed in Peter Steinke's research. These are not concerns that affect other people. They affect all people, our people in our pews. Worshipers may not come expecting specific answers to specific dilemmas, but they *do* expect integrity. They do expect the circle of God's blessing to somehow encompass their need. Pollyanna sermons that skate around tough realities do not fly. The sanctuary should live up to its name; it should be a safe place to embrace the myriad wounds of society. However, the issue here is ministry, not controversy. Sermons need not reflect tabloid and TV talk-show sensationalism to honestly, pastorally, and powerfully proclaim the good news of God's grace. Ironically, that proclamation is naming what is already present!

Announcing What *Is!*

David Schlafer says the primary business of preaching is to announce what is, rather than to hassle listeners about what *should* be,

> Preaching evokes our response more than it exhorts us to respond. . . . Those who hear the message of divine love will have to recognize it as already at work upon and within them. The preacher's task is to name what is already present, to evoke it, to call it forth, rather than to lay it on or crank it up.[14]

The Holy Spirit does not go on duty at eleven a.m. each Sunday and wrap it up at noon. God is constantly at work in the lives of people. Most Christians know this. All of them forget it. That is why we worship. Worship *is* memory. We worship to be reminded of the salvation acts that we already know, yet consistently forget. Worship opens us to the numinous within and without our being. It is a *kairos* happening, a moment when the eternal breaks in on the temporal and the temporal is prepared to receive it. It is an experience of lively awareness: a moment in time, but not governed by time, in which we remember the past, the present, and the future.

We remember God's benevolence and faithfulness within the scripts of our personal history. We have a vivid awareness of God's gift of an actualized present. That is, we experience the present moment free of competing voices that drown out our sense of being. It is a present that has fidelity only to itself. We experience the now of living and are reminded that demands on us in this moment can wait. In this actualized present we are reminded that it is enough just to be. We remember that the future is God's call to us and that prevenient grace precedes us into the unknown tomorrows. Worship as liberating memory releases us from the bondage of destructive relationships that *dis*member us from life! Through liberating memory we are *re*membered.

Preaching, then, as the sacrament of the word, evokes our response to that which is already at work in our lives. The old, old story becomes renewed in us. We remember that our God loves us and empowers us in our defeats and our victories. Schlafer would say that the preacher's role in this sense is not to tell them what they want to hear, but to tell them what they want to say!

"What do I preach?" is the blatant cry of the preacher straining for sermon ideas and inspiration. Name for the people what is already present. Help them say what they want to say. Surprise them with something they already know. Surprise them with joy, hope, love, and peace!

Surprised by Joy

The note of joy is sounded forcibly and lyrically throughout the scriptures. Someone once remarked, the music is so persistent it is like being in a bird sanctuary in the morning.

Remind your listeners that the road to the recovery of joy is not to say, "now I will be joyful," but to put yourself into the experiences that produce joy, receiving the unspeakable gift of God and taking up the cross. Remind that there is no joy in being brought forth alone, that their salvation and the salvation of others are inseparably connected. Help them say what they want to say, that Jesus calls us to mutuality: to be for God, for self, and for others. That our primary calling is not to be peculiar but to be like Jesus, and if in so doing we are peculiar, so be it!

Remind them that our calling is to live the life of joy found in worship that stretches beyond the sanctuary where the workbench, the office desk, and the dining room table become the extension of the Communion table. Help them say that joy is a matter of laying claim to Christ's victory, free of our feeble attempts to recompense God for it.

Surprised by Hope

Someone said that despair has three heads: *agnosticism*, which makes one lose courage in the search for knowledge; *pessimism*, which makes one lose courage in the search for progress; and *cynicism*, which makes one lose courage in the search for virtue. If there is one disease that is rampant in our time it is cynicism.

Surprise your hearers with hope! Remind them that Christ is our hope, because Christ finishes his sentences. Regardless of the seeming futility of life's unevenness. Regardless of unfairness. Regardless of the cruel twists of circumstance that may cast us adrift on an ocean of confusion, despair, heartache, or doubt we are not left dangling in mid-sentence, mid-thought, mid-crisis. Even when

God is silent, there will be a period, even an exclamation mark, after the pause or comma! We are not abandoned without sail or rudder. Jesus completes his sentences; he never reneges on his promises.

Refresh them with the power and hope of the gospel, the power of God to pick up our lives—no matter how much we have neglected them or smothered them or rejected them—and offer them back to us as gift. The real sin that many of us need to confess is our subtle decision to die, to not let anything new happen to us, and to just ride out our days instead of awaiting the new birthing God has for us.

Surprised by Love

Remind your listeners that

> neither death, nor life, nor angels, nor principalities, nor powers, nor things present, nor things to come, nor height, nor depth, nor any other creature, shall be able to separate us from the love of God, which is in Christ Jesus our Lord.—Romans 8:38–39

Remind them that although God's love is unconditional, it is not cheap. The sacrifice of Jesus sets a seal on the magnitude of that love.

Surprise them with love's obligation to live love. Remind them that love and acceptance are not synonyms; that God's love is a transforming love which does not accept the status quo. Tell them what they want to say—that love cares about the condition of the beloved and always seeks for one's highest good.

Surprised by Peace

Speak to them a word of peace in the midst of turmoil.

> Therefore, continue to be strong in faith. To you who hear my voice and know my promises I will reveal myself and give my peace, even in the midst of your uncertainties.—Doctrine and Covenants 158:11a

Remind them that peace has to do with personhood, not property, or comfort, or convenience, or ambience. Tell them peace is never only a negative state, never simply an absence of trouble. It is the peace of the actual rule of Christ's kingdom come, and will done, first in our hearts, and ultimately in the cosmos. Remind them that peace can never perform its function so long as it exists in splendid isolation. Tell them in their own words that *we* do not establish the kingdom, but we live as if the kingdom were already in our midst.

Podium or Playground?

"Mommy, can we please just pay the man and go home!" I began this chapter with that phrase and will conclude with it. If we have not heard this cry, we certainly have experienced it. I don't ever remember hearing, "Mommy, can't we stay, do we have to go home?" The polarity that separates these two responses is stretched out on a continuum between the pulpit which is treated as podium and one treated as a playground. Schlafer states that how we look at the pulpit is vital. Is it a podium, prison, or playground? I vote for the playground. This is not said flippantly. Nor am I referring to sheer use of the pulpit in terms of entertainment (although sermons should be entertaining–able to capture one's attention and imagination). I am referring rather to the need of the preacher to bring all available resources to create an alternative world. To do so requires a great deal of imagination, creativity, and inspiration. It demands the freedom to play with ideas, narratives, images, and arguments. Without the Spirit the music is dead. Pulpits that are podiums or prisons bind the Spirit.

Pulpits should be places for dialectical interaction, participation, drama, and performance that make real the vision, mission, and celebration of the gospel. The gospel presents a counterculture message of good news. It says, "Things don't have to remain the way that they are!" Positive preachers play in the pulpit. They put their best efforts to articulate the dream of how wonderful life can be when lived in Christian community, into God's hands.

In summary, positive preachers keep close to the Source. They know that without the Spirit the music *is* dead. They know they are involved in sacred conversation: the sacrament of the word. They listen before they speak. They plot where they want to go. They announce what is and what can be. They proclaim Jesus Christ. They promote joy, hope, love, and peace. And when they do so, preaching becomes a joyful and positive experience for listener and speaker!

Study Questions

1. The author says, "the divine encounter made possible by preaching (the sacrament of the Word) is no less valid than the rites we traditionally refer to as sacramental." Do you agree or disagree? Is there a difference between an ordinance and a sacrament? How can preaching be considered a "sacred conversation?"
2. Preaching is not a monologue. It is many voices. The author suggests that the secret of good preaching is response and refreshment. The preacher must have something important to say, must want desperately to say it, and must say it well. Discuss putting "first things, first!" What are your priorities for sermon preparation?
3. "Although the sermon may inform and educate, this is not its major objective. The sermon is not the place to do theology." How does one preach and not do theology? If the purpose of preaching is proclamation, what is it that must be proclaimed? Should a sermon be more descriptive than prescriptive? Discuss your understanding of the phrase "to preach is to be part of a dynamic event."
4. "Preachers should know their preaching context." What is meant by a "head-high . . . heart-deep sermon"? How does a preacher share his/her deep convictions without imposing his/her theology?
5. Considering the varied conflicts, dilemmas, moral and other issues confronting persons today, are there topics that should not be addressed from the pulpit?
6. What does the author suggest in stating that "worship is memory"?
7. What does it mean for a preacher to "name for them what is already present"?
8. What is your most memorable sermon experience? How did it influence you and why? What made it unforgettable? Name a preacher you admire. Why is he/she an effective preacher?

Notes

1. David J. Schlafer, *Surviving the Sermon: A Guide to Preaching for Those Who Have to Listen* (Boston: Cowley Publications, 1992), 3.
2. Thomas H. Troeger, *Imagining a Sermon* (Nashville, Tennessee: Abingdon Press, 1990), 137-138.
3. Schlafer, 116.
4. Ibid., 31.
5. Troeger, 71.
6. Schlafer, 22-24.
7. Phillips Brooks, Sermon: "The Candle of the Lord." (Further information unavailable.)
8. J. Randall Nichols, *Building the Word: The Dynamics of Communication and Preaching* (New York: Harper & Row, 1980), ix.
9. Eugene Lowry, *How to Preach a Parable: Designs for Narrative Sermons* (Nashville, Tennessee: Abingdon Press, 1989), 35.
10. Lewis Carroll, *Alice in Wonderland.*
11. Lowry, 173.
12. Tex Sample's book *Ministry in an Oral Culture: Living with Will Rogers, Uncle Remus and Minnie Pearl* will help preachers educated in the literate culture of academia bridge the culture gap between them and those in their congregation who verbalize their faith in proverbs and stories.
13. George Herbert, "The County Parson" (1652), as found in Richard Lischer, ed., *Theories of Preaching: Selected Readings in the Homiletical Tradition* (Durham, North Carolina: The Labyrinth Press, 1989), 51, as quoted by Thomas H. Troeger in *The Parable of Ten Preachers,* 81.
14. Schlafer, 28-29.

4

Honest Relationships

David D. Schaal

Suppose that Mary Magdalene had had no witness to her shame and she could have sneaked through life with honor and in death sneaked out of the world with a myrtle wreath upon her brow–it seems to me that through her courage she won another honor; it seems to me that in death she lies more honored without the myrtle wreath than with it.[1]

–Soren Kierkegaard

A Tale of Two Cities

Once upon a time, there were two villages nestled in the foothills of a great mountain range. The first village prided itself on the beauty of its architecture, its always-clean streets, and the sparkle of fresh paint that appeared to cover every home and shop. The village was even more proud, however, of the fine, upstanding morality of its citizens. There was no need for a jail (except for the occasional visitor who might cause trouble while passing through), and the only two remaining social workers spent the majority of their time directing youth programs for the well-behaved boys and girls who emerged out of the village's seemingly perfect homes.

At the center of the village square was a large statue of its founder, a tall strong pioneer whose eyes flashed brilliance and courage. On the pedestal of the statue, the pioneer's personal motto had been etched: "Truth, not lies!" These words had become the village motto as well, to the point where the telling of lies was considered to be the grossest of social ills, and everyone was expected to tell the truth. Political speeches within the village always quoted the village motto, and the valedictorian of each year's graduating class always reminded her peers of the heritage of truth-telling which their generation must uphold and perpetuate. Community celebrations were held often and usually included the affirmation that the citizenry was indeed fortunate to live in a village wherein the telling of truth and the avoidance of lies were not only primary values but the expected way of life.

Consequently, when someone purchased a piece of machinery and was told that it was in excellent working order, the buyer could rest assured that it was. When a restaurant owner proclaimed that her soup was made with only the freshest ingredients, her customers knew that it was so. When the village council and school board met, the accuracy of reports was never questioned, and the meetings were always conducted without conflict and with utmost politeness.

Lies were never heard in this little village, because telling the truth was of supreme importance–sort of.

You see, underneath the fresh paint and collective smiles there existed real people. Not everyone's children attended the youth programs directed by the two remaining social workers because not everyone fit in (especially the kids who "acted out" their anger and hurt which was accumulated from countless unknown circumstances). The man who sold the machinery always did so with a smile and a thank you, but no one in town knew of his personal hopes and dreams which really kept him going. While the fresh ingredients used by the restaurant owner were enjoyed by everyone, literally no one knew that on many occasions their vegetables had been washed by the cook's tears who did not know what to do about her overwhelming loneliness. It is true that the village council and school board meetings ran smoothly, but nobody ever spoke openly of their concern that decisions were being made for the many by the few, typically behind closed doors.

So it was in this first little village, where no one ever *told* a lie, and everyone smiled as they gathered together at the community picnic to extol the virtues of telling the truth.

The second village was different. It did not sparkle with the fresh paint of the first village, but it was clean (relatively) and was a pleasant place to be. The village had been founded by the same pioneer who had begun the first village, and his likeness stood in this village square as well, with the same words, "Truth, not lies!"

etched into the pedestal. (It was difficult to read the words, though, because village maintenance crews had used too strong of an acid the last two times that graffiti had been removed from the statue.)

In this village the youth program was well run, but not without conflict. Efforts were under way to involve as many kids as possible, even those from homes that were neither perfect nor healthy. Fighting was common, but the kids and their parents were frequently in conversation with the social workers and things were starting to work out. Village council and school board meetings were often places of intense discussion and frequent disagreement, yet all sides felt listened to most of the time, and there was a good feeling of working together (although Mr. and Mrs. Brown continued to be irritating to most people most of the time).

When the woman at the hardware store whistled while she worked, most people were reminded of the good fortune that had recently come into her life. On the other hand, when the grocery store clerk was a bit rude one day, it was understood that he was going through a rough time at home and really did not mean to hurt anyone's feelings. Civic speeches were not as polished as in the first village, but their focus was more on the realities of village life than platitudes and clichés. In short, this was a village where people fought and made up, laughed and cried, were disappointed and dreamed dreams.

Once upon a time there were two villages nestled away in the foothills of a great mountain range. Which one was the most *honest?*

This parable is a reminder to us that real honesty goes far beyond simply telling the truth. Honesty has to do with being genuine, which includes taking off the masks we wear and being human together. On an even deeper level, honesty has to do with living lives in which our words, actions, and lifestyles are aligned with the values we hold most dear.

In congregational life it is possible for us to become a genuine community of joy in which we are members of a close fellowship of friends and associates engaged together in a worthwhile mission. If such community is to be developed, though, it can only do so in an environment of interpersonal trust, and there can be no trustworthiness between people without the essential ingredient of *honesty*.

This chapter will explore three different aspects of honest relationships in congregational life: honesty with one's self, interpersonal honesty, and congregational honesty.

Honesty with One's Self

If we are to experience honesty in congregational living, we must learn to be honest with ourselves. If we are not honest with ourselves, then we cannot truly be honest with others because the person we present to them is only an image of who we are projecting ourselves to be at that moment.

At the same time, being honest with ourselves may be one of the most difficult things we have to do. I remember listening to my stereo one day at home when I decided to go downstairs for a moment to check on our children. My daughter was listening to country music in her room, and my son was listening to rock 'n' roll in his. As I walked down the stairs, the music from their two rooms and the music from my stereo upstairs all began to blend together so that my ears were filled with a tremendous mixture of sound–none of which was intelligible at that point. Likewise, our heads can be filled with a myriad of voices, each one competing for a portion of our attention, and each one telling us what we need to be accepted, "good", successful, or beautiful. These voices come from parents, friends, church, the media, family, culture, and countless other sources. As they sink into our conscious and subconscious mind, it is sometimes difficult to look honestly at ourselves and say, "This is what I *believe,*" "this is what I *want,*" "this is who *I am.*" In the midst of so many voices, learning how to be honest with ourselves is one of the great challenges of our faith journey.

What Do You Value?

Earlier it was said that real honesty goes beyond telling the truth and has to do with aligning our words, actions, and lifestyles with our deepest values. An initial consideration then, if we want to be honest with ourselves, is that of identifying what it is that we truly value. There are several ways to engage the question "What do I value?" They range from a simple consideration of the question to the use of more sophisticated values-clarification instruments. One simple way to begin looking at this matter is to experiment with the following exercise.[2]

Take the time to schedule about thirty minutes when you can be by yourself with little chance of interruption. (You will need a pen and three pieces of paper.) Once you are settled in your private space, use your imagination to pretend that you are going to a memorial service for a loved one who has just died. Imagine that you are sitting in the church or funeral home, noticing the gathering congregation, hearing the sounds and seeing the sights around you.

Gradually your awareness expands and you recognize that this service is taking place in the future–that it is five years from now and that the memorial service you are attending is your own. Sitting around you are the friends, family, and associates who have come to remember you. As you look at the order of worship, you notice that there are three speakers who are scheduled to address the congregation: A family member, a good friend, and an associate from work. Each has been asked to say something about you.

Now, take one piece of paper for each of these people, and write out what it is that you *hope* they would say about you.

After completing this exercise, review what you have written. Do your notes regarding how you hope to be remembered suggest anything about what you value? Are there other values you embrace that this exercise did not reveal? Which of your dearly held values are helping you to become an effective, whole, Christlike person?

Once we identify what we say we value, the next step is to take an honest look at our language and behavior. Do they align with what we say we hold dear, or are there significant incongruencies?

Several years ago, for example, my wife and I shared with a young couple about to be married. As we talked about marriage that evening, I boldly proclaimed the need to keep "courting" each other even after they were married. It was essential, I suggested, if the spirit of romance was to be kept alive in their relationship. After they left our home that evening, my wife turned to me and asked, "So when are *we* going out next?" As soon as she posed the question I realized it had been far too long since just she and I had been out on a "date." I had proclaimed a principle to our about-to-be-married friends, but I was not living it in my own life (until that next week, of course). In other words, my wife's gentle reminder helped me to realize that to be truly honest, I needed to live out what I said I valued.

Each of us, if we were to be truthful with ourselves, could identify areas of our life that are out of alignment with our most cherished values. The point, however, is not to feel guilty, but to continue to move our lives toward congruence with our cherished values. Along the way we will frequently stumble and fall, but it is the *attempt* at such congruent living that constitutes being honest with ourselves.

What Are Our Motivations?

One more item regarding being honest with one's self should be mentioned: What truly motivates us to do the things we do? I remember being verbally attacked by a minister in the church who had taken offense at some changes I was proposing for the way our congregation conducted its worship. As he criticized my ideas, he vehemently claimed that he was doing so only with the best interests of the congregation in mind. Further conversation, however, revealed that he saw himself as the congregation's "father/guardian" and deeply feared his role would change if others were allowed to participate in key worship planning roles. What was really motivating him was not the good of the congregation but the fear of having to redefine who he was. This did not make his critique of my ideas right or wrong; the issue was one of motivation.

Being honest with ourselves includes a willingness to take a look at what motivates us to say and do what we do. Every now and then, it is helpful to intentionally slow down, find a quiet place for a few minutes, and simply meditate on the question "Why do I *really* want to do this?" or "Why do I *really* say that to people?" The object is not to approach these questions analytically with "hard thinking." Rather, the point is to simply contemplate the question of what is motivating us to do or say certain things and see if anything interesting "bubbles up" into our awareness. Perhaps our conviction to act or speak in a certain way will be strengthened. Perhaps unacknowledged motivations will come to light.

Taking such a candid look at our motivations is hard work and should probably not be undertaken by those without a good sense of humor. Certainly it requires a degree of courage, the type of courage Paul Tillich reminds us "conquers the threat of guilt."[3] The courage to examine our motivation is, however, essential if we are to have an honest relationship with ourself.

Interpersonal Honesty

Our relationship with Jesus Christ is personal, but it is not intended to be private. While our spiritual journey is in some ways unique, it is nevertheless a journey that is meant to be shared in community. While there are many dimensions to the experience of community, honesty between its members is one of the great essentials. Specifically, we will examine two expressions of interpersonal honesty in this chapter.

Telling the Truth

Trust is built between people only if they find each other to be trust*worthy*. One sure way to erode trust is to be dishonest; one sure way to build trust is to be consistent in telling the truth. For just a moment, think of someone whose word you have counted on—when he or she tells you something, you simply know that person is telling you what is truly believed to be the truth. Now, think of others who have not been honest with you, perhaps sharing only half-truths with you to protect themselves or manipulate you. How would you compare these two relationships? Obviously, with one you feel safe and the most willing to risk with and open your life to. Just as obviously, the other type of relationship breeds secrecy, mistrust, and bitterness. In congregational life, honesty must be practiced over time for deep trust to develop.

Going a step further, interpersonal honesty in the congregation also has to do with being consistent. This does not mean we should never change our minds, but that we should strive to be free of duplicity. For example, several years ago I visited a congregation where the leadership council was involved in a spirited dispute over a particular proposal that was beginning to divide the congregation. One council member, who favored the proposal, was often approached by various individuals wishing to inquire about the subject. She calmly stated her opinions to whomever inquired, even if the inquirer was known to be on the "other side of the fence." A second council member, who also favored the proposal, was also approached frequently by people wanting to discuss the matter. This person, however, tended to say to the inquirer whatever it was they thought the inquirer wanted to hear. I will not comment on the result of the second council member's actions. I will say, however, that though the proposal did not carry, the first council member continued to be a respected and valued minister, largely because of her trustworthiness. Not only was she free of duplicity in what she shared, but more importantly, she was consistent in the integrity with which she listened and communicated.

If I am a different person with you than I am with others, how will you know when I am being myself? If, on the other hand, I stay true to my values no matter where I am, you may not agree with me, but you will be more likely to trust me.

Being Human Together

Once, at a reunion, a man approached me wanting to share a problem he was having in his personal life. As is often the case, he was reluctant to share the problem with his congregation for fear he would appear weak and then lose their respect. Not long after that, I was approached by a woman from a different congregation who was trying to pull her life together after a period of personal struggle. She had shared portions of her brokenness and subsequent struggle for wholeness with a few congregational members and felt as though they had been helpful in the evolution of her healing. This particular man and woman were different in many ways. But she lived in a congregation where it was acceptable to be *human;* in his, few people ever took off their masks. He felt alone in his struggle, while she felt included in a caring community.

Perhaps one of the most challenging aspects of honesty in congregational living is being human *together.* Congregations are made up of real people with real joys and hurts. It can be so easy to parade into church each Sunday morning, wearing practiced smiles and using properly pious language; underneath it all we (or the person next to us) may be the bearer of tremendous joy or awful pain.

The Christ we worship rejoiced, wept, touched, got angry, displayed gentleness, healed, and sweat blood in his disciples' presence. A central proclamation of Christianity is that **God chose to be human.** Why is it, then, that we sometimes avoid being human together? Perhaps we are fearful of appearing weak, of being judged by those whose acceptance and love we need. Whatever the case, it is often true that the church is closest to Christ when its members willingly open their lives to one another.

This is not to suggest we should "spill our guts" to the congregation every chance we get. It is to say that within the church, relationships should be developed in which people can express their joy, share their pain, confess their sins, and voice their hopes. These are expressions of living together honestly. Such relationships will not grow in environments that are judgmental or in gatherings where true acceptance depends on conformity within narrow margins of tolerance.

When teaching classes on welcoming visitors I often ask the congregation, "Is this a friendly, accepting congregation?" In almost every circumstance, the majority of the participants have strongly affirmed their congregation as friendly and accepting. Likewise, there is almost always a smaller number of people who, when the question is asked, simply stare at the floor and say nothing. I have discovered that this smaller group typically comprises those who are in some way "different" from the rest of the group, whether by age, gender, race, socioeconomics, or theological position. In almost every case, though, as we explored the matter further, we discovered that the majority had no idea this group was feeling marginalized. We also learned that those who were feeling left out typically had not revealed their feelings. Likewise, many of those in the "mainline" of church life have often mentioned they long for relationships in which they can be who they really are, rather than feeling the pressure to only self-reveal what their congregation wants them to be. The bizarre part is that, in some congregations, that is everyone's secret wish.

Being honest in our relationships calls us to risk a bit in revealing our humanness. Likewise, it calls us to handle with gentle care those who open their lives. This means we may have to learn how to cry together *and* how to celebrate together as never before as we experience the joy and struggle of honest relationships.

Congregational Honesty

Congregations are not simply collections of programs or people. A congregation is a living organism with a personality and life of its own. The messages that congregations send to their members and community can be powerful. Consequently, the matter of honesty becomes a corporate as well as a personal and interpersonal matter.

Being Honest about Who We Are

Not long ago, I had the opportunity to visit two congregations on the same day. One was a small, rural congregation with an average attendance of about fifteen, located in a shrinking little town of about 200 people. The other was a congregation with an average attendance of about 150, in a metropolitan area of more than 400,000. In addition to size and location, the two congregations also differed significantly in their socioeconomic makeup, the needs of their members and their communities, and their overall congregational personality.

This being the case, one might expect to discover that these two congregations had different worship styles, different program emphases, and different ways of organizing their leadership structure. I was amazed, however, to discover that both congregations had adopted a list of officers, program emphases (at least on paper), and worship styles that were remarkably similar. It was as though a great voice had spoken and said, "There is only one way for proper RLDS congregations to look." The result was that both congregations were attempting to fit into a preconceived mold of what they thought "church" should be, even though it was not congruent with their gifts, circumstances, and personalities. Just as individuals who are honest with themselves will attempt to "be who they really are," so should congregations.

Members and friends of the RLDS Church are fortunate to be associated within a denominational fellowship that provides resources and suggestions for congregational living. It is not intended, though, that all RLDS congregations should have the same slate of officers, run all the same programs, or adopt the same style of worship. Certainly World Church policies and guidelines need to be honored, but within those guidelines and policies there is significant freedom for congregations to "be what they need to be" in line with their unique strengths and circumstances.

Being honest with ourselves as a congregation includes a willingness to take an open-minded look at our strengths and weaknesses. It also implies that we will not attempt to be something we are not presently in a position to be. Instead, we will build on our strengths and be honest about who we are.

It is a faithful way to give corporate expression to the Doctrine and Covenants affirmation: "All are called according to the gifts of God unto them . . ." (Doctrine and Covenants 119:8). This is as true for congregations as individuals. To ignore this advice and attempt to be something we are not condemns our congregations to ineffectiveness at best and irrelevance at worst.

For instance, imagine a congregation with about thirty active members that is uniquely situated and gifted to minister to neighborhood children and their parents. Let's also assume they have very few (if any) gifted public speakers. If this congregation is to respond "according to the gifts of God unto them," then perhaps it would not be wise for them to adopt a system that includes eight commissions and preaching every Sunday. Maybe they would be better off to articulate their vision, invest their energies in only a few things (revolving around ministry to children and their parents), and employ a worship style that is more relational and less dependent on formal preaching. Would this not be a more honest expression of who they are?

The good news in all this is that congregations do not have to feel guilty just because they cannot staff a large choir, have eight fully active commissions, or be just like some other congregation that is supposedly ideal. Honesty means being who we are–personally and congregationally.

The scriptural story that comes to mind is David and Goliath. When David volunteered to face the giant Philistine, the king did what was expected by outfitting David with the traditional apparel of a warrior. The only problem: none of it fit and poor David could hardly walk around in it, let alone go into battle! Finally, David shed the ill-fitting armor and armed himself with the weapons that naturally fit *him:* a sling and several smooth stones. If David had been concerned about looking like every other warrior, he would have stumbled onto the battlefield unable to lift his arms under the weight of his oversized garb. Likewise, some congregations are weakened because they operate under the burden of trying to fit a particular mold when, in reality, they are called to be who they are.

So how can your congregation take an honest look at itself? One way is to explore three particular questions.

The first question is, "What are the most significant needs of our members and attending friends?" The issue here is not necessarily what our most pressing "religious" needs are, but our most significant needs as human beings (a sense of belonging, stress reduction, help with family matters, a sense of God's nearness, etc.).

The second question is, "What is the mission of this congregation to our community?" It may be helpful to pretend that none of your current programs exist and that you are considering this matter for the first time. It will also be helpful if you avoid general answers such as "It's our mission to serve Jesus" or "build Zion." A more specific expression would be appropriate, such as "provide ministry to community children" or "care for the poor in our city."

The third question can be both fun and extremely difficult: "What would our congregation look like if we built our worship and program totally around the responses given to questions one and two?" What kinds of things would we do together? What would our worship look like, sound like, feel like? When and where would we meet?*

When most congregations explore this third question seriously they typically end up confronting two realities. One is that there are usually some dimensions of congregational life that are relevant to the real needs and mission of the people.

The second reality, though, is the awareness that some of what we do in the congregation is relevant neither to our needs nor our mission. Congregational honesty calls us then to talk together about how we can bring what we actually do as a church into alignment with our needs and mission. This is hard interpersonal work, and it is extremely difficult to do in congregations where the trust level is low, or where a small handful of people feel a need to "broker" all the decisions. In congregations where the relationships are healthy, though, this can be an empowering exercise of honest sharing and planning.

Delivering What We Promise

Keeping our promises is obviously a vital expression of personal honesty. It is just as essential for congregations, which tend to

---

* These questions are best discussed when ample time is given for their exploration over a period of several days or weeks, versus a quick treatment of them during a solitary one-hour session.

make promises (or at least state claims for themselves) more often than they realize.

I have a friend who attends a congregation where a young woman was baptized several years ago. This particular young woman was a very pleasant individual, even though her life contained a litany of pain from a series of unhealthy and destructive relationships. At the time of her first contact with the church, her lifestyle was far afield from what the local congregation would consider healthy or moral. She was in deep need of love, of belonging, and the experience of doing something worthwhile; when she came into contact with the church, that is exactly what she was promised. She heard preachers proclaim the church as the "family of God" where love was lived, and visiting ministers in her home spoke with her about the cause of Zion, wherein a person could actually work together with God and others in making a difference in the world. What a wonderful thing it was when she discovered that what she had heard was true. The congregation did accept her and love her. In addition, congregational leaders helped her discover opportunities to serve in meaningful ways. In sum, the congregation was true to its word.

Consider this kind of congregational honesty for a moment. When the church both testifies of what it is called to be *and* actually lives it, it is a powerful experience. On the other hand, if people are forever hearing language in the congregation about love, caring, and impacting their world for good, but never see the congregation actually doing these things, then such phrases become little more than hollow words. In fact, if after a period of time the congregation's actions remain incongruent with its words, then people simply will become numb to the high-sounding language and the church becomes little more than a motion that we go through. Trust is also diminished, because we apparently do not believe what we are saying or we would be doing something about it.

Of course the church is not perfect. Of course those of us who make up the church will frequently fall short of the ideals that we uphold. Nevertheless the question remains, Are we attempting in our congregational lives to live out what we proclaim? It is far better to honestly confess our sins as disciples who try, occasionally fail, but keep on trying, than it is to spout altruistic phrases that never quite sink into our hearts, hands, and feet.

Do we proclaim love and acceptance? Then the congregation should not be a place of undue judgment and critique. Do we affirm that God loves the world? Then, if we are living honestly, we will be engaged in missionary witnessing and in concrete efforts to improve the quality of life in our community. As in personal honesty, congregational honesty also has to do with bringing our words, actions, and values into alignment. When this occurs—and it often does—the result is the unleashing of relevant and powerful ministry.

Jesus said the kingdom is like a pearl of great value; so valuable that when one finds it, he or she sells everything they own to obtain the pearl. There are countless numbers of boys, girls, women, and men who are relationally and spiritually destitute because they have not yet discovered this "pearl." The call of congregational living is to create the kind of environment wherein people have the possibility of making this discovery. Such an environment must have honest relationships as a primary characteristic. When looked at in this light, honest congregational relationships are not only vital for nurturing trust, but they become the building blocks that help make the church a place where lives are opened to the kingdom of God.

Study Questions

1. What are the major influences that have affected what you value? Have these values been healthy or unhealthy?
2. Why is it important to "slow down" and be intentional about exploring our personal motivations?
3. What are some of the risks of taking off our masks and "being human"? What are some of the potential blessings?
4. How would you describe your congregation's "corporate personality"? What are your congregation's greatest strengths? What are some of its weaknesses?
5. No one and no congregation is perfect, but to what degree do the relationships and programs in your congregation match what is proclaimed in worship?
6. What are some specific ways you and others in the congregation can help people discover "the pearl"?

Notes

1. Soren Kierkegaard, *Stages on Life's Way,* ed. and trans. by Howard and Edna Hong (Princeton, New Jersey: Princeton University Press, 1988), 353-354.
2. This exercise has been used in a variety of forms by many people. One helpful use is found in Stephen R. Covey's *The 7 Habits of Highly Effective People* (New York: Simon and Schuster, 1989), 96-97.
3. Paul Tillich, *The Courage to Be* (New Haven, Connecticut: Yale University Press, 1952), 116.

5

Deep Caring

Richard D. Hughes

Several years ago as a child, my sister, Donna, was placed in a hospital for children as a result of a nearly fatal illness. When she recovered, her school mates had been promoted on without her. Donna's reading and spelling skills had not been nurtured during her sickness.

Mabel, a schoolteacher in our home congregation, heard about Donna's reading and spelling difficulty and made a long-term commitment to help. Three times each week Mabel picked up my sister before 7:00 a.m., took Donna to her home, and tutored her. Mabel then dropped Donna off at school before driving on to the school where she taught.

These tutoring sessions were a great help to Donna, because her lack of reading skills hindered learning and were an embarrassment to her. Mabel did not have to develop that reading program for Donna. She did it because she cared deeply for a child of God.

Jesus Cared Supremely

Mabel learned about caring from her family and church members. She learned early in life that Jesus loves everybody.

Jesus is reported to have told his disciples, "the greatest love is shown when a person lays down his life for his friends . . ." (John 15:13 Living Bible). This comment was made in the context of Christ's teaching about love.

Jesus stated,

> I have loved you even as the Father has loved me. Live within my love. When you obey me you are living in my love, just as I obey my Father and live in his

> love. I have told you this so that you will be filled with joy. Yes, your cup of joy will overflow! I demand that you love each other as much as I love you.—John 15:9–12 LB

Christ's disciples heard in no uncertain terms that they were called to love deeply. These same words call all of Christ's disciples to love deeply. Mabel heard that call when she cared so deeply about my sister almost fifty years ago.

Deep Caring

When we love deeply, we care deeply. Deep caring extends far below the surface of our lives. Deep caring encompasses the height, depth, and breadth of our experience.

Recently a popular "radio psychologist" made a distinction between relationships of convenience and commitment. Relationships based on commitment, she said, tend to be lasting, deeply felt, solid in good and bad times, and exhibit love as an underlying component. In contrast, relationships of convenience tend to dissolve or disintegrate when things become "inconvenient." There is no glue to hold the relationship together—no deep caring.

When Christ calls us to *love* one another, he is doing more than asking us to *like* one another. When we love one another, we share some of the caring attributes: tolerance, kindness, compassion, mercy, forgiveness, sacrifice, long-suffering, and forbearance.

Deep caring has been exhibited throughout the ages. People have heroically extended themselves or their groups so that others might have a better chance at life.

We are all aware of the parable of the good Samaritan. This expression of caring went far beyond bandaging the wounded. The good Samaritan took care of the robbery victim's immediate and future needs in a courageous manner. He made a deep commitment to the poor wounded soul.

Like the good Samaritan, deep caring requires a basic commitment to the individual, family, or group that needs help. If we help someone and then "drop them cold" when the situation gets difficult, the person needing help may become even more deeply wounded than they already are.

Sometimes we are called on to help others because we are the first ones to stumble across them in their time of need. At other times we may observe a long-standing need that has not been met. At such times, we need to think twice before walking away.

If we decide to share the gift of our lives with others, we would be wise to ask ourselves some questions about the specific situation:

1. How long are you willing to commit yourself to this specific need? Will you be required to commit yourself and your resources for a day, a week, or a lifetime? If you are adopting a child, you will be expected to love and care deeply for the rest of your life. If you are caring for a child for a week, you may be called on to give intensely for a short while. When you give your time and talent, you are giving a part of your life for that person or group of people. You are demonstrating your own "greater love."

2. Is your immediate family willing to support you in this deep-caring experience? If your family does not support your kindness, the experience could sour for you, the person you are caring for, and your family. You must ask yourself if you have a right to commit for others who may not be as committed to the project. One way to ascertain the support of others is through a family council, a congregational meeting, or a "feeling out" of all those involved. This is also a good way to gain support for the project.

3. What will be the cost in terms of time and resources? Will it require use of the spare bedroom, another mouth to feed, gas for the car, or time involvement? If you *shortchange* the person being helped, he or she could feel devastated when turned away because of a lack of continued resources.

4. Could a social agency do a better job? Are you equipped to help a drug abuser or would it be better to see to it that the person in need gets the required professional help? If you try to minister to someone in a way you are not fully qualified, is it possibile you could be preventing the one in need from getting help?

5. A related question: Will you be helping or getting in the way of needed help? If you counsel a married couple that has great needs, but you yourself have no skills in marriage counseling, will you be keeping the couple from getting the counseling they really need? Will you, while meaning well, give "help" that does more damage than good? In such a situation, it would be better to assist the couple to find a competent counselor.

6. If you commit yourself deeply, how will you find renewal? If you burn out, what will happen to the person you are caring for?

Indeed, what will happen to you if you get so tired that you will not say yes again?

One of the sad lessons often learned too late is that people need renewal. Sometimes wonderful people withhold their talents because they gave until they were "dry." Caregivers need care, too. Those suffering burnout are often highly motivated, idealistic people who seek to give until it hurts.

Of course, when we undertake deep caring, we often do not think of the consequences. Our hearts overflow with love or duty toward other people or good causes.

When I look back on my life, I realize that repeatedly I have been blessed by people who cared deeply. They were my church school teachers, coaches, neighbors, coworkers, and sometimes strangers. Within a few feet of you in your congregation are usually many people who love deeply and give deeply.

Situation 1

Don and Pat are typical of the folks I've been privileged to share with in the church. Pat was a beautician. Don was a corrections worker. Pat saved her tips each year so she could donate money to the reunion, whether she attended or not. They were both always helping someone.

As retirement time drew near, Pat and Don decided they wanted to help people who could not help themselves and who, in fact, could not even thank them for the help.

Don and Pat enrolled in a hospice training program so they could offer their love and tenderness to those who would soon die. In this way Don and Pat have continued to share their deep love for others through service.

Situation 2

An African-American family joined the local church congregation, which was mostly Caucasian. The church people considered themselves a family and took in their new family members without any hesitancy. They loved the new family. Over the years, most of the children in that congregation prepared to attend college. This caring congregation wanted to support their children's ambitions and so developed a grant program to encourage and support their youth as they sought to obtain additional education.

The young African-American man wanted to attend college, but he did not have enough monetary resources to allow him to enroll. One of the caring Saints in the congregation gave this young man a job and helped pay his way through college. This kind of love is an example of the body of Christ in action.

Situation 3

A nonmember junior high girl attended church with her church member friend. As a result of the fellowship and love she found there, Debbie accepted Christ and was baptized.

Debbie's background was a difficult one. A couple of years after her baptism Debbie became pregnant out of wedlock. She knew the church did not sanction premarital sex, but she could not hide the reality of the life growing within her.

The women of the congregation, without "preaching" to Debbie, gave her a baby shower. They taught her how to care for the newborn child. Some even gave Debbie an occasional day off from the responsibilities of child care so she could shop or just rest.

Debbie always loved those people and that congregation. She was able to turn her difficult situation into a more normal life because the women of that congregation had cared deeply for her.

Situation 4

Art and Dick, two ministers from a local congregation, learned that a nearby county hospital had a floor for the very elderly who were unable to care for themselves. These patients had no worship services available to them, and so the hospital requested Art and Dick to conduct Wednesday evening services.

When Art and Dick took the request to the local congregation, the people decided to hold services for the hospital on a weekly basis. Eventually the whole stake began to participate in the program. Each month a different congregation conducted the services. Each week several Saints pushed the people in their wheelchairs to the services, after which they pushed them all back again.

The original two ministers developed a fund for the confined elderly of the hospital, some who were wards of the state. On one occasion they bought leg braces for an individual who became increasingly crippled and had no funds for the braces. On another occasion they hired a special van so a severely crippled woman could attend her father's funeral in a faraway town. They even occasionally baptized some of their flock.

One of the ministers, Brother Dick, who was more than eighty years old at the time, confided to me that this ministry was the most joyful and meaningful ministry of his life. Both Dick and Art have passed on, but the ministry they started continues to thrive.

Situation 5

Two brothers, about ages ten and twelve, were placed in a children's home several states away from their community. Their mother had died, and their father, who worked for the armed forces, was unable to care for them. The boys were church members.

The oldest boy contacted the local congregation in the area where they were sent to live. The Saints responded positively to the smiles and good nature of the two boys. Each week a different family from the congregation would pick the boys up for church and take them home for dinner afterward. Some of the congregation attended the athletic and band events in which the boys participated. These young men eventually graduated from high school with honors, attended Graceland, and later became professionals.

As adults, both of these men became intensely involved in the ministry of Christ and have held major offices in the church. The people of that small congregation knew how to share their love. They cared deeply.

Situation 6

Mary and Paul fell deeply in love as young people. Throughout their married lives they supported their local congregation. They made friends and served wherever they could.

Their happy union was not blessed by any children. However, they loved their niece, other family members, and church member friends.

Before Paul died, the couple prearranged that all their resources would be left to Mary. Mary continued to worship and serve in her church family.

When Mary passed on, she remembered her family by leaving some assets to them. But her deep caring for the members of the congregation became even more evident when word came that she had left more than half of her estate to the church in an endowment fund.

Mary and Paul planned to leave funds so that the interest from the endowment could help the church carry out its mission. They cared deeply about the church. Their resources will continue to minister to people who will be born years from now.

Deep Joy

As stated previously, deep caring often requires much sacrifice on the part of the caregiver. Sometimes caregivers have "second thoughts" about whether their help will make any difference, or whether "it is all worthwhile." Sometimes caregivers learn to be more tolerant, more long-suffering. Helping deeply, by its nature, often takes sacrificial living.

However, all is not giving. Often deep joy is a part of deep caring. When you sense accomplishment in a commitment well done, or when you know that you did the best you could under the circumstances, you are able to feel satisfaction, or even deep joy.

When we feel deeply, we may not want to laugh or shout. Something inside us wells up. We may even be overcome by tears, or become speechless. But we know in those moments of deep joy that we are living in harmony with what we believe to be the will of God.

Examples such as those in this chapter could be multiplied by the millions. All of us have witnessed deep caring. Most of us have cared deeply on many occasions.

The call of Christ to us present-day disciples is much like the advice Jesus gave to Simon Peter by the lake of Gennesaret. "Launch out into the deep, and let down your nets for a draught. . . . And when they had done this, they enclosed a great multitude of fishes . . ." (Luke 5:4–6 IV).

Study Questions

1. Relationships of convenience and relationships of commitment are fundamentally different. How would each type of relationship relate to deep caring?
2. Give illustrations or testimonies of some deep caring you have known about in your experience. Were the projects easy ones? How long did they take?
3. What is meant when the author states that people must ask themselves if they have a right to commit for others who may not feel the same level of commitment? What are some possible outcomes of "imposed commitments"?
4. Sometimes people who mean well can make a bad situation worse by trying to help. Can you give examples of this type of bad experience? If we do not have the skills to help, but someone comes to us for help, what should our response be?
5. Do you know of cases of "burnout" in the church? Do not use names, but you may discuss how the burnout could have been prevented.
6. Have you ever felt deep joy? Share your experience. Describe how you felt.
7. Read John 15:9–12. According to this scripture, under what circumstances will people find deep joy?
8. Are people ever too young or too old to care deeply? How does maturity affect our deep caring?

6

Communication as Ministry

Linda L. Booth

"I communicate. Everyone communicates," you say. "So why do I need to take time out of my busy life to read about communication? I have more pressing responsibilities, like making sure our congregation's budget is met and finding someone to head the Christian education department."

Well, before you flip pages to the next chapter, if you think a discussion of communication isn't important, consider this: You may have the most inspired vision, the most caring mission statement, and hope for the most enthusiastic community celebration, but all your planning will fail unless you know how to listen and communicate with others.

In fact, it is my experience that thoughtful communication creates a powerful sense of community and makes leadership responsibilities less stressful and more joyful. As communication creates an environment where people feel part of the church family, worship appears more inspired, pastoral care becomes a natural response to community, volunteering for ministry responsibilities happens frequently, and budget goals are exceeded because people freely give.

Communicating effectively is more than a skill or tool. It is a healing, caring, loving ministry. When you view communication as ministry, listening and conveying provide immeasurable blessings and activate the Spirit in people's lives. Communication as ministry unites, informs, encourages, and inspires people. It creates a sense of family, nurtures, loves, and prepares individuals to share the good news with others.

If communication is not viewed as ministry, listening and conveying may be discounted or overlooked as unimportant. As a result church members can become separated, misinformed, discouraged, and bored. Without thoughtful communication, vision is squelched, mission comes to a screeching halt, and celebration bombs.

The ministry of communication doesn't just happen. It takes well-thought-out plans. To illustrate how this works, let me share my own experience as a congregational leader. For the past four years, I have used a communications plan as I served as the pastor of the Olathe, Kansas, Branch. I am not suggesting that my plan will work for you. Every situation is different, and I encourage you to tailor a plan to fit your congregation's needs or your area of responsibility. Whether you are a youth leader, worship committee chair, or the pastor, any or all of the following ideas can be molded to fit your ministry situation.

Internal Communication–within the congregation

Two-Way Communication

Listening	*Conveying*
Focus groups	Newsletters
Leadership team	Share & Care
One-to-one	Bulletins
Monthly congregational meetings	Special flyers/letters
Nip-it-in-the-bud	Personal communication
	Calling chain
	Gathering opportunities
	Greeters
	Pictorial directory

External Communication–within the community

Newspaper briefs
"Welcome to the church" signage
Community/Church Alliances
Yellow pages & advertising

Internal Communication

Listening

Communication is more than speaking or relaying a message. Effective communication goes two ways: from listening to others to sharing information with everyone.

The most effective communicators listen as well as speak, just as Jesus did. Jesus stopped to listen to people the disciples thought unworthy or insignificant. In the nineteenth chapter of Matthew, the disciples rebuked the parents who brought their children to Jesus. They thought Jesus had better things to do than listen to the parents' needs. But Jesus listened and blessed the children, bringing ministry and support to the whole community.

By listening to people as Christ did, you let members of the community of Christ know that what they feel, think, and believe is important to you and to the church. They realize their ideas and input are valued, and you want them to be active in achieving the mission of the church. Members feel empowered and encouraged to discover, cultivate, and use their gifts in a caring church home.

The following ideas will help you hear the voices of the people you serve.

• **Focus Groups.** When I became pastor, I realized that even though I had been a member of the Olathe congregation for sixteen years, I really didn't know how others felt about important church matters. So I telephoned every adult in the congregation and personally invited them into my home. I asked them to bring a dessert to share and told them I needed their input and direction.

For two months, three nights a week, eight to ten people sat in my living room. I started each focus group with a prayer, asking that the Spirit grace our fellowship. As we ate dessert, we caught up on what was happening in each family. I then asked each group the same questions, telling them that there were no right or wrong answers and that their feelings and thoughts were important. The questions focused on worship, Christian education, and fellowship. Groups were asked what they thought was working and how we could make improvements in each area. I took notes as they talked. I shared with them my hopes for our congregation, and then we joined hands and ended with a circle prayer.

As a result of these focus groups, several positive things happened:

• People got excited about the coming year.

• Many ideas for programs and events were generated.

• People who might not normally have volunteered or been asked volunteered for a variety of ministry responsibilities.

• Each person realized I cared for them because I had taken the time to invite them into my home and listen to them.

• These discussions eventually became the basis for our congregation's vision and mission statements.

• **Leadership Team.** You are not the only person in your congregation responsible for listening. In fact, any leader who thinks he or she can do it all is setting themselves up for failure. Your responsibility is to train and encourage others to listen. Encourage your leadership team to listen to those they work with and to see themselves as pastors.

Well-publicized monthly meetings are critical. Allow time at each meeting for team leaders to report on their area of responsibility. Listening to each other's ministry plans and scheduled events creates a supportive environment and helps everyone to see how they fit into the big picture. We found that ministry areas began to work together, supporting other programs with their talents and expertise.

I tried to take time for frequent one-to-one conversations with team leaders over breakfast or lunch, to celebrate their joys and support them in their times of stress. Never let your leadership team members feel isolated. If you do not help them deal with their personal needs, their frustrations or anger will spill over into congregational life and cause separations. Don't forget to notice their body language as well as their words.

• **One-to-one Communication.** Encourage your church family members to call you or a member of your leadership team with concerns, needs, or ideas. During my four years as pastor, I received many telephone calls and talked to a lot of people over lunch or in the church foyer. No one took advantage of my open-door policy. In fact, as I loved them, they took particular care to love me back and protect my family time.

Don't argue with those you don't agree with. Listen to them, acknowledge their beliefs or feelings, and in a loving, sensitive way, let them know that while you may disagree, you respect and value their opinions.

Encourage people to tell you about themselves. Learn about their interests and giftedness, and then match these interests and gifts with ministry responsibilities. There are more successes and less burnout in congregations when we listen to what people want to do as contributing members of the church family.

• **Monthly Congregational Meetings.** Choose a different topic to discuss each month. However, make sure you are willing to listen and act on people's suggestions so they feel their time is well spent in attending the meetings. Invite and encourage input by all ages. We have had meetings, for example, on adopting a room in the Olathe Salvation Army's homeless shelter and on hiring a full-time pastor.

At one monthly congregational meeting each member was asked to walk through the church building with a clipboard and take notes on what improvements needed to be made. A lively discussion followed with many suggestions, including replacing our 1970s orange carpet, lightening up the walls in the sanctuary, putting larger mirrors in the upstairs bathrooms, and building a large storage room off the gymnasium.

These suggestions launched our Rebuild '90s Program and generated a lot of enthusiasm. They helped the building committee determine remodeling priorities, which then began a major three-year fundraising program that raised more than $40,000.

• **Nip-It-in-the-Bud.** If you're listening, you will discover and stop problems within the church family before they get out of hand. Never ignore rumors or problems that are brought to your attention. If you do nothing, these rumors and disagreements between people or groups will fester and spill over into all areas of congregational life.

One day I received a call from a woman who told me that the wife of a member of the pastoral leadership team had told her that her husband was upset with me. I was tempted to ignore this report because I had that day talked with the man, and it was obvious we had a healthy relationship.

But I knew I couldn't ignore her conversation because it was probably being repeated to other people. So I got up my courage and called the man's wife, who could be quite cutting in her remarks. I asked her to tell me about her thoughts and feelings. For about ten minutes she complained that I had not supported her husband in a situation concerning several families. When she finished venting her feelings, I patiently tried to explain to her that because her husband and I had disagreed about how to handle the situation that did not mean I did not support him. I told her how much I appreciated his ministry and friendship, how much I loved her and her family, and how important her support was to me and to our church family.

She cried, and I cried. And healing came to both of us. If I had not listened and met this problem head on, I know our relationship would have been hurt, and other people could have been brought into the situation to take sides.

Conveying

In today's information-rich, computer-literate world, it is often difficult to communicate with church members. Our time is limited. Everyone is busy with work and family responsibilities. And with the constant information bombardment from junk mail to e-mail, people may miss the church messages we're trying to give them because they are overloaded with too much information.

In a time when life was less complicated, several announcements in the church bulletin might have conveyed the news you're trying to share. Today, people need to hear and read the same announcement several times before it sticks in their minds. Even our church attendance makes it harder to communicate. With people traveling more because of business and family responsibilities, consecutive Sunday attendance may be unusual in your congregation.

When creating a communication plan for a program or congregational event consider the following:

1. First decide who is your target audience. Who you are trying to reach may determine how you relay the message. For example, if you are planning a friendship banquet for adults, you may communicate in different ways than if you are trying to get the word out about a pizza party for junior high youth.

2. Make a list of all the ways you might reach your targeted audience, such as bulletin inserts with eye-catching graphics printed on colored paper; announcements made before the church service; colorful posters created by children and hung on the church's front door or along the hallways; lunch or breakfast meetings;

chalk messages written on the church sidewalk; announcements made at planning sessions or priesthood meetings; mailed formal or informal invitations; monthly newsletter articles; specially designed flyers mailed to the home; telephone calls; handwritten notes; or letters from the pastor or leaders.

3. Use the at-least-five rule. Communicate your message a minimum of five times, preferably in five different ways. For example, if you want church members to attend a business meeting,

- send out a letter announcing the date and time;
- put preliminary budget items on the agenda at a congregational planning session, leadership meeting, or priesthood gathering;
- run the announcement four or five Sundays in the bulletin;
- highlight the meeting in the monthly newsletter;
- on the four preceding Sundays, make announcements before the Sunday services;
- mail out the budget information, agenda, and resolutions a week or two before the meeting; and
- personally tell people it's important they attend.

Communications Vehicles

The following communications vehicles are important to any plan.

Monthly newsletters unite people in the sharing of the news and events important to the church family. They are best created by people who sense a calling to bring ministry in this way. Humor and love need to filter through all articles.

Determine who should receive the newsletter, such as

- active and inactive church members
- friends who have moved away
- college students or members in military service
- community leaders
- visitors

Newsletters are an excellent way to keep inactive people aware of what's going on so when they do come back to church, they will still feel part of what's going on.

What should be included in the newsletter? This question will be answered differently by each congregation because of their membership needs and interests.

The *Olathe Branch Observer* always includes
• a letter from the pastor
• a calendar of events
• profile of an adult and a youth
• reports from the leadership team
• book steward report
• grapevine—news about church family members
• prayer concerns
• movie reviews, recipes, etc.
• seasonal information, such as about graduates and holiday news

Our newsletter is mailed using the bulk mail rate.

Greeter. Stationing someone by the church entrances and encouraging them to talk with the incoming people communicates a welcome and starts the worship process. Greeters are often Aaronic ministers who ask about what's happening in the family and individual's lives. People are asked to volunteer for greeting ministry and then placed on a three-month cycle.

Share & Care occurs at the beginning of the worship service and celebrates church family good news and presents needs and prayer concerns. The selection of the Share & Care person is important. The person selected should have a caring attitude, smile easily, and realize he or she will not only share news but help lead people into God's presence. He or she needs pastoral care and speaking gifts.

Before the service, the Share & Care person stands in the foyer and collects information to be shared at the worship service.

Share & Care is listed in the bulletin as part of our worship experience. The "Share" portion includes highlights of upcoming events and good news about members of our church family. For example, we applaud children who make the honor role or lose a first tooth, adults who get a new job or discover they're pregnant. There's a lot of interaction between the Share & Care person and the congregation.

As a transition to the "Care" portion, we sing a "Welcome to the Family" song, and then prayer concerns are shared. Share & Care is followed by a moment of silence, and then the worship service continues.

Bulletins. Events and important information are most effectively remembered when the items in the bulletin run for several weeks. Bulletins should be considered a worship tool and reflect Christ's gift of joy and grace to the community. They should include details for upcoming events (event, date, time, place, cost, etc.), prayer concerns, and the names and telephone numbers of the pastor and leadership team, if appropriate.

Special Flyers/Letters. Even though some events have been listed in the bulletin and highlighted in Share & Care for several weeks, it may take a special letter or flyer about that informational meeting or special program to get a good turnout.

Our worship committee has also sent out special packets to help people prepare for Advent and Easter seasons. Packets included a worship calendar, the worship themes and explanations, and stories and scriptures to be used in individual or family worship. These packets were computer designed, wrapped in bright paper, and mailed to all families. Many people commented that the packets enriched their worship experiences.

Personal Invitations and Notes. Remember, personal communication is the most effective communication. While printed communication is important, nothing gets results like a personal phone call, a conversation over lunch, or talking with someone face-to-face. Personal communication is especially important to get new members involved and feeling like a part of the church family.

Don't forget to communicate your appreciation for ministry given or a job well done. Often we forget how important it is to tell someone "thank you" or that we love them and appreciate their friendship. For some people, your hug, smile, or caring words may be just the encouragement they need to continue doing God's work.

In our congregation, we communicate our joy and support during family milestones and sorrows. One person is assigned to send birthday cards to everyone on our church rolls and notes of support or congratulations for the birth of a baby, a death in the family, graduation ceremonies, or a move to a new home. Flowers or helium balloons are sent to those hospitalized.

Calling Chain. Every church family experiences crisis or prayer concerns that need to be communicated quickly. Our congregation has a calling chain set up like a tree. The chain is only used for emergencies and is initiated by the pastor. Those responsible for the Calling Chain realize they are asked to bring ministry and are given a detailed list of who to call with up-to-date phone numbers.

Pictorial Church Directories. Because our congregation is large, every three or four years we try to publish a pictorial church directory so people can link faces with names. This is a difficult endeavor. We've used members' talents to take photographs and schedule photo sessions. We've also used church directory businesses to produce the directory. Either way, the pictorial directories have been a blessing, especially to integrate new families into the congregation and help them feel at home.

Gathering Opportunities. Fellowship activities may not be considered communication—but they are! Anytime you provide an opportunity for people to get together to share what's happening in their lives, you are bringing a most thoughtful communication ministry.

Some fellowship opportunities that have worked well for our church family are:

• *Dinners*—once a month a family cooks a meal for the entire congregation. Tickets are sold, and people enjoy sitting around and talking without the hassle of bringing and warming up potluck dishes.

• *Monthly adult/family socials.* One favorite adult social is our yearly "Not-So-Newly-Wed Game" and banquet. After a catered meal, we gather for a hilarious spoof on the Newlywed Game. Newly married and long-time married couples are asked questions, and we all laugh and have fun with their answers.

• *Birthday party for the whole congregation.* People whose birthdays fall in the same month sit together. Someone is assigned to decorate the table and bake and decorate a cake using that month's theme. Children and adults alike enjoy this event.

• *Workdays.* Working side by side provides a unique opportunity to catch up on what's happening in everyone's lives.

• *Support and interest groups,* such as football, movie video, and study groups, meet once a month to enjoy each other and their common interests.

External Communication

The early church grew because people believed they had something unique to share with others. As a maturing church we realize that while we share the truths of the gospel with many other denominations, we still have something wonderful to share with our friends, neighbors, and community: the message of Jesus Christ and warm, caring church families.

There are many people who feel isolated and alone and need people who will love and nurture them. They need a church family that will help them discover their gifts of ministry. They need a church where they can experience with others the Spirit's presence.

There are many ways you can tell community members about what you have to offer:

1. Many newspapers will publish short articles, "briefs," about what's going on in your church. These briefs can give what, when, why, where information about a variety of events happening at your church: guest speakers, vacation church school, and youth canoe trips, for example.
2. Church/Ministerial Alliances provide an opportunity to allow other church leaders to know about the good things you are accomplishing in your church and in the community.
3. Your local Chamber of Commerce often provides a listing of churches to new families moving into the area. Call the chamber and make sure your congregation is included.
4. Make sure your church grounds are inviting and that a "Welcome, Visitors" sign is prominently displayed on your church lawn.
5. Run an ad in your local newspaper, or at the very least make sure you have a listing in the white and yellow pages of your telephone directory.

Good communication, both listening and conveying, internal and external, is more than publicity. Publicity promotes an event or disseminates information. Communication in a congregation brings ministry, creates community, builds family, and unites people in Christ's love.

The best communicators share the good news with others with an attitude of joy and celebration. And through that sharing, relationships with one another and the Christ are strengthened. People are then better able to go forth, renewed in God's love, and excited to share God's message of hope, peace, and love with others.

Study Questions

1. Give examples of how thoughtful communication brings ministry.
2. Give examples of times when thoughtless communication has caused hurt feelings or estrangement.
3. Discuss examples when Christ listened and then conveyed a positive message to others.
4. Brainstorm about all the ways you communicate information to church members.
5. Choose an upcoming event, and create a communication plan to get the word out. Use a minimum of five communication strategies to ensure that people respond to your message.

7

Compassionate Service

Cathleen D. Cackler-Veazey

What do you think of when you hear the term "compassionate service"? Do you see images of self-sacrifice and devotion to the needs of others? Do you think of people like Mother Teresa or Mahatma Gandhi? Perhaps you think of someone closer–a parent, minister, or friend–as the model of such servanthood. Most Christians consider Jesus Christ to be the first and most important compassionate servant.

Compassion and service *are* closely related, but when they are considered separately, we may be able to glimpse a clearer picture of what compassionate service is all about. The word "compassion" comes from the Latin words *com* and *pati*, which together mean "to suffer with." Compassion calls us to be with those who are in need, to hunger with those who are hungry, to weep with those who cry out in desperation and frustration. Compassion is the feeling that causes us to share another's pain and to suffer with the hopeless.

Human experience shows us that compassion is usually not the natural response society has to the problems of life. Not everyone feels that the weak and poor should be cared for by the strong and wealthy. Many in society are conditioned to ignore those in need and to praise those whose success has brought them material wealth, even if acquired at the expense of the disadvantaged. Greed and self-interest are the opposites of compassion, but they are often considered valuable assets in the competitive world of today.

We are taught to find our identity through achievement as we ascend to the top of this or that profession, and we often do so in a way that isolates us from others, especially those outside our social group or economic class. This separation keeps us from seeing the real needs that surround us. With these blinders on, we often find little reason even to justify our indifference to the poor and broken. Such a system encourages people to set aside their compassionate feelings by appealing to the darker side of human experience.

So how do we become compassionate people despite such societal messages? Those who want to see compassion in the flesh must look to the example of Jesus Christ. Through the life of Christ we see God's intention for us. We see what it means to suffer with others, and to make their burdens our burdens. God is with us when we act in a caring way toward others. And when we do, we open ourselves to a closer and more intimate relationship with God, who is the embodiment of compassion.

Jesus demonstrated compassion for those in need many times throughout his ministry. One of those times was at the pool at Bethesda. The scriptures tell the story of the man who had lain for many years trying to be the first into the pool when the waters moved. The belief was that angels occasionally touched the waters of the pool, causing the waters to stir. When the waters moved, it was thought that the first person into the pool was healed. The man by the pool was so crippled and slow that he could never be first into the water, so he lay year after year until one day Jesus came by. Seeing and having compassion on the man, Jesus asked him if he really wanted to be healed, thus enabling the man to be a willing participant in the compassionate act that was about to happen. The man said yes, accepting Jesus' gift of healing and the beginning of his new life.

Service is the activity that expresses compassion. Jesus exemplified this by taking action when someone in need reached out. Such service confronts those social mores that ignore the needy and place self first, with the call to put others first. Service can be done only in relationship to others. When done with the quality of humility, it is a demonstration of the best that one can offer. Throughout the scriptures, and especially in the life of Christ, there is manifestation of the importance of the service-centered life. The concept of servanthood is mentioned more than twenty-eight times in the New Testament. The best known of these references is John 13:4–17 where Jesus washed his disciples' feet. This portrayal was an act of humility that so impressed the disciples that they were awestruck. This lesson, learned that day in the upper room, was to be a guiding principle of the Christian movement. We are to serve one another as Jesus served.

Compassionate service is rooted in being with those in need in ways that demonstrate the message of Jesus Christ. We are to stand in intentional, self-sacrificial ways with those who suffer. In accepting this concept, we are challenged to identify practical actions through which such a commitment to service is lived out. It is, therefore, important to consider some simple processes and guidelines through which compassionate service can be made visible in our lives and the lives of those around us.

Becoming Service Oriented

When we decide to become compassionate servants, a process begins that changes life. Such a decision can require us to change in many ways. The first change involves **hearing the call** to be something different from before. It may come as a gentle, quiet voice from within or through a major life-changing event. But regardless of how the call comes, we feel the need to choose a new way of going about life. Jesus called his disciples to be different from what they had been. They became an elite group, the closest to the Master—the inner circle. Yet Jesus called them to be servants. He asked that they wash the feet of the lowly, that they accept as equals the women of the street, the unclean, and the tax collectors. This call was difficult to answer and required major life changes. These disciples were never the same again.

A second change, closely following the sense of call, is the need to **envision what compassionate service means** and where it can lead. This visioning process is what directs future service activities. Some would say this means dreaming the dream. It involves glimpsing what can be if we respond to the call. Sometimes visioning does not mean setting new goals but rekindling old dreams that have not been fulfilled. Many are the well-intentioned journeys that are waylaid. To vision is to look at the mountaintop from the valley below and decide to go there.

Compassionate service may begin with a simple act and result in a trip to the mountain. Mother Teresa's work began with the desire to help a few of the destitute in the streets of Calcutta. But as one step leads to another on a journey to the mountain, so one act leads to another for Mother Teresa. Her work is now world renowned, and the basis for a great ministry.

Any journey starts with a certain amount of preparation. To begin the journey of compassionate service, we will need to take along several things:

Faith is first. God is always there, but faith opens the door for God to enter our hearts and lives. Search the scriptures and other good books for guidance as faith develops.

Hope strengthens the resolve and makes the beginning possible. The journey that anticipates the possible is one that is filled with hope. Hope is what makes possible the realization of the dream.

Love prepares the heart for those times that are difficult when serving others. Not all that is experienced in service to others is easy or pleasant. But when servanthood is begun with love for those who are being served and for God, compassion replaces resentment.

Willingness to suffer for the sake of others is another essential element as we anticipate our journey of compassionate service. When serving those who have experienced brokenness, it is difficult *not* to be touched. We often resurrect our own pain when we assist others in dealing with theirs. Most among us have experienced hurts along life's road. Those experiences can strengthen us and make us more able to understand and thus serve others. But past hurts also make us more vulnerable. Sharing stories bonds people to one another. Doors are opened by the willingness to share our vulnerability with those being served. Our readiness to suffer with others by facing our own pain allows us to serve humbly and in a more meaningful way.

Sometimes suffering with others means taking on their life experience and making it our own. Gandhi learned that to serve others, he had to become like them. He changed his lifestyle, clothing, and personal habits to be among the people. A story is told of a mother who brought her son to Gandhi, asking that he tell the boy to stop eating sugar. Gandhi replied that they should go and return in a week. When they did, Gandhi looked at the boy and said, "Stop eating sugar." The mother thanked Gandhi, but said, "Why did we have to wait a week for you to tell my boy that?" Gandhi replied, "Before I could tell your son to stop eating sugar, I first had to stop eating it myself." Compassionate service calls us not only to offer ministry, but to become one with those with whom we minister.

Putting others first is the essence of loving. Perhaps Francis of Assisi put it best in his prayer:

> Lord, make me an instrument of Your peace;
> where there is hatred, let me sow love;
> where there is injury, pardon;
> where there is doubt, faith;
> where there is despair, hope;
> where there is darkness, light;
> and where there is sadness, joy.
> O Divine Master,
> grant that I may not so much seek
> to be consoled as to console;
> to be understood as to understand;
> to be loved as to love.
> For it is in giving that we receive;
> it is in pardoning that we are pardoned;
> and it is in dying that we are born to eternal life.[1]

The cost of living out the ideas that Francis of Assisi expressed has a price. Such a lifestyle is not popular because it makes those not living in such ways uncomfortable by focusing on what community with others should be. That is not the way one "gets ahead" in a world where power is more important than compassion. Assisi's thoughts, in contrast, are an expression of compassionate service as demonstrated in the life of Christ.

The process of becoming a compassionate servant begins when we hear the call, envision the journey, and accept the costs of suffering with those in need. The successful journey begins with these elements and is modeled after the example of Christ.

Guidelines for Service

As we seek to live lives of compassionate service, there are principles that can assist in the process.

First, it is important to accept that "Acting with compassion is not doing good because we think we ought to. It is being drawn to action by heart-felt passion."[2] If we serve for reasons other than a desire to serve God and others, and without a passion for the activity, the service will not last long or truly serve those in need.

Second, compassionate service should begin in a spirit of prayer that opens us to God's direction. When considering the call to service, use contemplative prayer to seek God's help. While searching for avenues of service, be open to the surrounding possibilities. The need may be close at hand, merely overlooked because of its familiarity. Be open to the stirring of God's voice in answer to the question, "Where can I give service?"

Third, the development of the following personal characteristics can assure that compassionate service is richer and more meaningful.

- Humility
- Honesty
- Unselfishness
- Forgiveness and forgetfulness
- Intimacy
- Skills

Fourth, as we develop these characteristics, it is also important to learn our limitations. No one can be served if the task requires skills that are not within the capability of the servant. Sometimes it is more loving to offer to step back and allow another, more able person to offer the service that is needed. This demonstration of humility and honesty relieves all those involved from feeling that they must have all the answers or all the gifts required to meet the needs of others.

Finally, it is important to remember to ask if our service is appropriate in the following ways:

- Is it in harmony with my values?
- Does it use my skills, talents, and personality characteristics?
- Does it make use of my opportunities?
- Does it acknowledge my liabilities as well as my assets?
- Does it take into account my existing responsibilities?[3]

Steps of Compassionate Service

There are some additional points that complete one's journey of compassionate servanthood. Some of these points are an expansion of ideas already presented; others are new.

1. Know yourself–gifts, talents, and resources. Act from the heart; know what you are capable of and what your resources are. Look at the need honestly and analyze your ability to address it. Be willing to grow but do not place yourself in a situation that encourages failure. Ask for help from others, using their gifts and talents in concert with your own. It may be better not to begin than to fail when success was not possible.

2. Listen—take time to be quiet and listen to yourself, others, and God. Look for opportunities for each of these to speak to you. Take a walk in the woods, pray in an empty church, take time to share with another where there are no distractions. Listening fully is the basis for compassionate service. Listen for the truth when making the decision to act. Listen for feelings when serving the one in need. Listen for the still, small voice of God when searching for the answer.

3. Start small—great deeds usually start with small acts. What community or individual need are you aware of? Find a small way to start addressing it. Say to yourself, "The way I really want to help is . . . ." Then begin to find ways to turn your statement into an action. Be yourself; find *your* place to serve.

4. Start where you are—you are the expert on the needs where you are. Look around and see with new eyes. Are there those who need your compassion? Look at your place of work, your church, your neighborhood, your family or friends. Are they places where you can offer your service? Perhaps there are needs not being addressed in any other way. How can you help?

5. Do your homework—now that you have learned more about yourself and your ability to give service, and you have identified needs that you want to address in ways that are attainable, research what others have done to succeed in similar situations. Learn about service techniques that have worked for others, about ways to address the needs of the disadvantaged and poor, or about new ways to approach community problems. Use the success of others as a model for addressing the needs you have identified. Talk to people in other churches, nonprofit groups, and service organizations in your search for new ideas. Most of all, keep an open mind for all possibilities to provide compassionate service.

6. Envision what you would like life to be—the vision is what directs us as we discover new horizons. Think about the kind of world you would like to live in and begin to take the steps to make it so. The vision is what gives us the conviction to do what has not been done before. Let the vision be your guide in compassionate service.

7. Be sensitive to the needs of others—first, get to know others so you can respond appropriately. Being a compassionate servant means putting their needs above your own. Analyze your motivation, study the life-experience of those to be served, and focus on the areas that will help meet the need most.

Compassionate service has been referred to as a journey toward completeness. When our lives are self-centered we miss the true call of Christian living. Jesus demonstrated through word and deed the importance of being a servant to others. Love is the basis of compassionate service, and love is the foundation of the gospel. Each of us is called to be a compassionate servant as we follow the example of Christ.

Study Questions

1. How is compassionate service viewed in your community? Give examples of acts of compassion by those in your church or community. Are these activities that could be models for further action?
2. Why does the process of becoming a compassionate servant require introspection and study?
3. Explore the importance of hearing the call and discovering the vision before beginning a service activity.
4. Discuss the seven characteristics of servanthood and why their development is important as one embarks on compassionate service.
5. Why is it important to consider the appropriateness of an act of service (see the list of five under Guidelines for Service)? Are there additional elements that should be considered?
6. Review the steps toward compassionate service. Discuss why the steps are important, and offer personal examples of when they have been useful tools in a service experience.
7. Develop a plan of action for doing compassionate service as a group. Identify a need and a method of addressing it, along with a time line for beginning. Follow the guidelines in the chapter as the service project is approached.

Notes

1. James McGinnis, *Journey into Compassion: A Spirituality for the Long Haul* (New York: Orbis Books, 1993), 31.
2. Ram Dass and Mirabai Bush, *Compassion in Action: Setting Out on the Path of Service* (New York: Bell Tower, 1992), 4.
3. Ibid., 136.

8

Full-Life Stewardship

Larry R. and Sharon K. Norris

The power of the prophetic words, "Stewardship is the *response* of *my* people to the ministry of my Son," is universal yet intimate. Response for us has become synonymous with stewardship. We have found that full-life *response* often generates such intimate involvement in the lives of others that those who respond have to move beyond what is simply known into the realm of mystery. Mystery can emerge as we try to deal with what appears to be simple reality.

Intimate response cannot only touch others deeply but can touch our own hearts as well. When community life is based on freely giving and receiving, each of us is called to give unreservedly. But even as we do this faithfully for many years, we can be confronted with the nagging expectation that surely life will eventually end its demands on us for response and we can rest and be relieved. In moments like this, one finds there really is no joy to be found in retirement from life. The good news is that life never ends, and with this realization also comes the awareness that the call to give and to receive is universal, something from which we can never retire. Response to the known, the unknown, the hoped for, the now, the already, the happy, the sad "is required alike of all those who seek to build the kingdom."

Our family has been blessed in many ways. In fact, our marriage has prompted some friends to tell us we have a "fairy tale" marriage. We have to admit, for many years it appeared to us that most of our dreams were becoming realities, and we seldom had hurdles that weren't quickly overcome. We had a wonderful relationship, and we had been blessed with our hoped-for precious children,

Ryan and Kamie. We were happily active as a family in church work, and we didn't have heavy burdens to worry us. Life was good and we were full of joy!

But then our dreams were shattered.

On August 17, 1993, our son, Ryan, took his own life at the age of twenty while in the depths of clinical depression. His illness had quickly consumed him. Our family immediately ached with the pain of emptiness, and all joy seemed to be drained from us. We would miss Ryan's presence on this earth forever. Our lives were changed, and we knew we would never be the same again.

Life is an ever-changing experience. We understood that then and we understand it now. But when you lose a loved one, it seems as if nothing will ever be right again. And it is in this realization that the pain of continuing to live life makes you feel you will never experience life's fullness again.

In David Bosch's book, *Transforming Mission,* he refers to the Japanese pictograph for "crisis" as being a combination of the characters for danger and opportunity (or promise). He affirms that

> crisis is therefore not the end of opportunity but in reality only its beginning, the point where danger and opportunity meet, where the future is in the balance and where events can go either way.[1]

People approach life in different ways. Some focus on remembering "the glorious days of the past" and ignore present realities. Others look to the future, constantly hoping for better days ahead and avoiding the present work that might assure future possibilities. A Catholic priest once said in a Communion message that every event in life is a transformational blessing. But in times of grief, disappointment, and sorrow it is hard to see the value of terms like "transformational" or "blessing."

It is true that through all the changing circumstances of life, things are never the same tomorrow. In the midst of great pain and tragedy, we struggle to believe that this changing future is a good thing or that we will ever again be comfortable with life and able to move forward to hope and assurance. But in more stable moments of quiet reflection, we realize that even though the changes that occur can hurt us deeply, we really would not want a static world in which nothing ever changed.

> Suffering itself has no value. It is the use that one makes of suffering. . . . Through attitude and action—therein lies the value. . . . Through the power of love, sorrow can deepen the soul in its capacity for joy—and the two can strangely coexist.[2]

The recognition that every person suffers loss and pain helps us understand the meaning of the Book of Mormon passage that teaches about opposition in all things and the contrast that gives meaning between bitter and sweet (II Nephi 1:98).

At the time of Ryan's death, we were richly blessed by another family who had also lost a child to premature death. They told us how they had discovered that joy is not the absence of suffering but the presence of God. God is the one who stands with us in mysterious ways, not only through outward expressions of the Spirit, but in tangible gifts of grace seen in people who share at times of need.

Even when we lash out in anger at God because we find it impossible to understand and to intellectually deal with severe pain, God is still there. The warm, comforting presence of the Holy Spirit repeatedly turns our hearts away from anger as it lifts us, sustains us, and implants in our hearts the hope and promise of future life and joy.

Stephen Covey indicates that the "quality of life depends on what happens in the space between stimulus and response."[3] Viktor Frankl, the Austrian psychotherapist who was imprisoned by the Nazis in the death camps during World War II, understood what this phrase meant. In his book, *Man's Search for Meaning*, he indicates that the only freedom that cannot be removed from us is the freedom to choose how we will respond to the experiences of life.

Full-life stewards understand that constant learning and changing are required as a steward's response to the marvelous and mysterious existence of life. The challenges of life are made of stimuli from outside ourselves and stimuli we create. It is the way we respond to these stimuli that determines our true freedom.

Traditionally, we have known this freedom by the name "agency." It is in the exercise of this marvelous and precious gift from God that deep joy may be found. Freedom of response is crucial to full-life stewardship, but this does not mean we can be arrogantly independent, assuming we alone control our own destiny. Instead, being a steward calls us to recognize that we are interdependent with God, others, and the entire created order.

The beauty of the gospel message is that life never ends. The present is of equal value with the past and the future in allowing us to learn how to be stewards who respond. Living fully in the present gives us the opportunity to live a life of gratitude for the past that we know and to live a life of expectation and wonder when we consider the future that is yet unknown.

The power of our gratitude for past blessings is most fully demonstrated when we respond in community to people in pain, and is the best antidote for the loneliness of spirit described by Dag Hammarskjöld. He is said to have indicated that what turns loneliness into anguish is not that you have no one to bear your burden, but that you have only your own burden to bear. Hammarskjöld is telling us that it is only within the caring community of those who hold a stewardship for life and for each other that the healing essential for wholeness can in love be born.

Robert K. Greenleaf has written,

> Love is an undefinable term, and its manifestations are both subtle and infinite. But it begins, I believe, with one absolute condition: unlimited liability of love! As soon as one's liability for another is qualified to any degree, love is diminished by that much. . . . Living in community as one's basic involvement will generate an exportable surplus of love which the individual may carry into his many involvements. . . .[4]

Joy that emerges from this kind of love is described in the scriptures in the response of the Macedonian saints to the needs of those in Jerusalem whom the apostle Paul had called on them to help:

> During a severe ordeal of affliction, their abundant joy and their extreme poverty have overflowed in a wealth of generosity on their part.
>
> —II Corinthians 8:2 NRSV

What power is found in the ministries of true community! This style of interdependent living comes about when a group of people are so committed to each other that they live life as a response to the goodness they find in each living and breathing soul.

As humans we are called to live in a spirit of commitment to one thing or another. And it is that one thing to which we commit ourselves that ultimately gives us our identity and our reason to live. As Abraham Heschel says, we become what we think of ourselves.

What we become in life is largely determined by our image of the "good life." If our primary focus is on assuring ease and comfort in life, almost as if we are in a comfort contest to see how many things we may be able to accumulate and how much free time we might be able to have, then our actions will focus on serving self and we miss the wonderful possibilities of interdependent living. But it is at the times when we are confronted with our need for the support and caring of others that the nature of the generosity of God in making us social creatures becomes the most clear. We know that we were not made to be rugged individuals who have little concern for or regard concerning others. Particularly at times of stress, pain, and sorrow we see the folly of "building more barns" rather than investing in others. But before long, we can find ourselves being drawn back onto the road of comfort and ease as if there is some type of cosmic dispute between the awareness of life as purely physical and the awareness that "spirit and element inseparably connected bringeth a fullness."

Karl Barth writes about this challenge in describing the spirit of Wolfgang Mozart's music:

> The sun shines but does not blind, does not burn nor consume. Heaven arches over the earth but it does not weigh it down, it does not crush or devour it. Hence earth remains earth, with no need to maintain itself in a titanic revolt against heaven. Granted, darkness, chaos, death and hell do appear, but not for a moment are they allowed to prevail.[5]

The journey toward full-life stewardship unfolds as we turn outward. Joy is found in a life lived in service to others.

> Service is the virtue that distinguished the great of all times and which they will be remembered by. It places a mark of nobility upon its disciples. It is the dividing line which separates the two great groups of the world–those who help and those who hinder–those who lift and those who lean–those who contribute and those who only consume. How much better it is to give than to receive. Service in any form is comely and beautiful. To give encouragement, to impart sympathy, to show interest, to banish fear, to build self-confidence and awaken hope in the hearts of others, in short–to love them and to show it–is to render the most precious service.[6]

One of the dangers inherent in any discussion of service is the possibility of ignoring the awareness that service goes two ways. There may even appear to be a contradiction as we realize that in addition to serving others, we also need to be served and to develop a gracious spirit of receiving. In our family's experience, we have personally found the need to accept and receive service during times of pain and grief. The fullness of life is discovered in service, through our willingness to receive the generous gifts of care, support, and service offered to us by others.

This realization calls us to move beyond reliance of laws and rules in determining the parameters of our full-life stewardship and to embrace the fundamental human desire to be a giver. When we do accept this understanding, we can live as givers who are eternally grateful for the magnificence and totality of God's creation even though we cannot fully understand and comprehend all of what that means.

Every person and creature with which we share this universe is a part of that mystery of life and, therefore, deserves our respect, attention, and care. We are called to be intimate with life. God becomes personal to us as we share personally with others in the created order. This is not to suggest that there is room for private religion that cannot stand up in the face of the questions and probings of the community of fellow travelers.

Barbara Evans, when visiting the Temple, made a presentation in which she indicated that the ministry of presence involves people being called to be the "necessary angel" for others. When we see ourselves as such we begin to look for and expect opportunities for ministry to come our way. When we feel the promptings of the Spirit calling us to offer ministry to another, we are thrilled to know that we are called and able to go and serve. Gratitude, thanksgiving, generosity, and joy are the hallmarks of a life lived to give. According to Henri Nouwen:

> We become beautiful people when we give whatever we can give: a smile, a handshake, a kiss, an embrace, a word of love, a present, a part of our life... all of our life. One of the most moving experiences of life is the experience of giving. . . . Our humanity comes to its fullest bloom in giving. . . . But I don't know of anyone who is really happy because of what he or she has. True joy, happiness and inner peace comes from giving of ourselves to others. A happy life is a life for others.[9]

Gary Beebe, at the memorial service for Ryan, told us that God can be trusted. Those words resounded in our ears as he repeated them three times very forcefully. We have reflected on his courage to share those words at a time when it would have been easy to assume that those experiencing our pain might have some question about the trustworthiness of God. Today, we stand to testify that God is faithful. There is nothing more faithful than to promise that life will never end and to know that God trusts us with the gospel, the "Good News." God also trusts us with the lives of those with whom we live day in and day out, and calls us to share the *breadth* and *depth* of the gospel in our relationships together.

Theadore S. Horvath wrote in a chapter titled, "Stewards of Life," that the same Greek word for stewardship *oikonomia* is used by Paul and his fellow missionaries to mean God's plan of salvation for humankind. It is invigorating to hear that as stewards, as people who respond in unqualified gratitude to the ministry of Jesus Christ, we are living God's plan of salvation. Paul goes on to indicate that as an apostle he had been given "the stewardship of God's grace" (Ephesians 3:2 RSV). The author of I Peter exhorts that all Christians are urged to employ their gifts "as good stewards of God's varied grace" (I Peter 4:10).

We believe that life is worth living to its fullest. Somehow, in a mysterious way, the sorrow and sadness that touches every human life is a necessary part of the fullness of life that we all share. Joy is found as we live life to its fullest; no single event or occurrence can finally destroy the ultimate joy found in sharing both on this earth as well as in the life after. We must not be caught in the trap of hoping to live here forever, or being anxious or excited about moving to the life hereafter. Instead, we are called to be absolutely and fully grateful for the present and to know that we have the complete freedom and trust of the great I AM as we choose how we will respond this day and every day of our lives.

According to the Book of Mormon humans exist "that they might have joy" (II Nephi 1:115). Joy is found in the presence of God, into which we come as we offer a life of service and generosity.

We thank God for the gift of Ryan. We know we are better people for having had him in our family, even though his time on earth seemed too brief for us. We also know Ryan wants us to feel joy, to continue to have new and different dreams, and to live lives in response to the ministry of Christ.

We are convinced that Ryan is pleased with the tremendous joy and hope that our loving daughter, Kamie, and our perfect little granddaughter, Cali Ryanna, have given to us. What a special blessing for us to have another precious child in our family! We also know that Ryan supports us as we have found opportunities to respond through educating and supporting others who suffer from depression, suicidal ideation, and grief. Our own pain is transformed each time we let God's love work through us as we help someone else. Even though life will never be the same without Ryan, life never ends, and someday we will all be together again. Until then, Ryan continues to live in our hearts, as we respond with joy and hope in new and different ways.

Truly life beckons us to "count it all joy." A full life of stewardship response includes the acceptance of the mysterious, unspeakable gift of wholeness represented in the life and death of Jesus Christ. A full life never ends and yet never will be the same tomorrow as today. A whole life embraces happiness and sorrow, service and being served, time and eternity. It also affirms the immensity and diversity of creation. All these things show us God's unfailing love. We are called to respond with unqualified love and service, forever.

Study Questions

1. Why would the authors indicate that "retirement from life" and "life never ends" are incompatible?
2. Identify a time when you knew life would never be the same. How did you feel and, in reflection, how did you respond?
3. Do you see service as what you do for others? How can you be of service by being the one receiving ministry?
4. How can joy embrace pain and happiness? Have you ever experienced that kind of joy?
5. Is there really such a thing as an "unlimited liability of love" as identified by Robert Greenleaf? Have you ever witnessed it?
6. What do you think Apostle Paul meant by "stewards of the mysteries of God" and the translation of stewardship as "God's plan of salvation"?
7. How can God be trusted? Do you think God trusts us?
8. What does "full-life stewardship" mean to you as a result of reading this chapter? Are there new understandings that you believe will have an impact on your life?

Notes

1. David Jacobus Bosch, *Transforming Mission* (New York: Orbis Books,1991), 3.
2. Alla Renee Bozarth, *A Journey Through Grief* (Minneapolis, Minnesota: CompCare Publishers, 1990).
3. Stephen R. Covey, Roger A. Merrill, and Rebecca A. Merrill, *First Things First* (New York: Simon & Schuster, 1994), 167.
4. Robert K. Greenleaf, *The Servant as Leader* (Minneapolis, Minnesota: Robert K. Greenleaf Center, 1970), 1973.
5. Karl Barth, *Wolfgang Amadeus Mozart* (Grand Rapids, Michigan: William B. Eerdmans Publishing Company, 1986).
6. Bryant S. Hinckley, *Not By Bread Alone* (Salt Lake City, Utah: Bookcraft,1955), 25.
7. Henri J. M. Nouwen, *Life of the Beloved* (New York: Crossroad, 1992).

9

Energetic Witnessing

Matthew C. Naylor

Christian ethicist James B. Nelson, in a discussion of sexual ethics in his excellent book *Body Theology,* tells the following story.

> A friend of mine, in the same profession as I, told me of an experience of his. He sat down next to a stranger in an airplane one day, and soon the two of them began to chat. Immediately, the other asked him that predictable man-type question, "What do you do for a living?" My friend replied: "I teach Christian ethics in a seminary." To which the other responded: "Christian ethics? That must be pretty simple. 'Love your neighbor as yourself'—I suppose that's all there is to it, isn't that right?" My friend thought a moment and replied, "Well, yes, I guess that's true. And what do you do for a living?" The other rather proudly said, "I am an astronomer." To which my friend responded (in one of his finer moments), "You are an astronomer. That must be rather simple. 'Twinkle, twinkle, little star'—I suppose that's about all there is to it."[1]

There is a tendency within Christian circles to respond to the matter of witnessing with a similar attitude to that illustrated in the preceding quote. It is not uncommon within the Christian media, particularly in the United States, and even within circles concerned with missionary work, to hear the admonition for witnessing presented in a manner that makes it appear straightforward and easy.

I suggest that effective witnessing is not a simple set of techniques or strategies such as you might use to sell any product. Energetic witnessing is not an in-home meeting where the gospel is sold or even displayed in a way that resembles the sale of plastic wear or household cleaning products. Effective witnessing is the result of a life lived *being* a disciple and has little to do with *doing* anything. It is when our lives are engaged in working with the needy and those on the margins of society that our witness becomes authentic. While some would have us believe that there is a technique for effective and energetic witnessing, I suggest that living a life deeply rooted in service to others is the only strategy from which true witness grows.

Loving Others

In my earlier years, I used to take a perverse delight in meeting members of a certain religious group soliciting people on the street. They would approach and ask if I would like to participate in a survey. The real intent of the "survey" was to have me go back to their offices around the corner, where I would be offered an opportunity to take a personality test and be exposed to their teachings. When these religious workers approached me they would invite me to participate in their study by answering three simple questions. But instead of answering their questions, I would ask them questions about their research method.

"Oh really, a study," I would respond. "What methodology are you using? What are the research hypotheses you are testing? How are you analyzing the results?" The religious workers would often stammer and get confused, because they were being taken outside the parameters of the script they knew so well. Then I would take great delight in telling them that I knew they really were not researchers conducting a study but were using surreptitious means to get me into their territory to present their philosophical and religious system. Such methods, I would say loudly, trying to attract as many passers-by as possible, were both dishonest and illegitimate. The presentation of truth never needs deception or manipulation to get a hearing.

On various other occasions I have been approached by well-meaning Christians who have asked me if I was saved. This has usually happened on a university campus and the approaches were well meaning. However, when asked what it means to be saved, these witnesses usually found themselves outside their scripted technique and unable to respond.

Contrast these approaches to witnessing with another that I discovered in the ministry of Lawndale Community Church on the south side of Chicago. Lawndale began its ministry in a neighborhood where there were more than a hundred liquor stores and not one supermarket. This neighborhood was filled with abandoned buildings; businesses had long moved out; no health care was anywhere near; and the churches were less than full.

A small group of people began a ministry which not only proclaimed what they defined as biblical Christianity but also provided relevant responses to the needs of those in the community.

Lawndale Community Church is a nondenominational ministry with a Sunday attendance of about a hundred people. But that is only part of what they do. Their ministries include the Lawndale Christian Health Center, which provides full medical and dental services every day; educational ministries, including tutoring and computer skills, basic reading, and math classes; and leadership development, whose goal is to raise a new generation of black Christian leadership for the community. They also offer college ministry which provides funding to people to attend college and builds a support system when they enter college and after they graduate; youth ministry, working with gangs, community service projects, and recreational ministries; and housing ministry—perhaps their most dynamic ministry—which buys up abandoned buildings and, using local tradespeople, renovates them for low-income families to rent or buy.

The reason Lawndale Community Church exists is not just to tell people about the gospel, but to show them the gospel through the provision of housing, educational programs, health care, economic development, and much more. These ministries bear witness to a transforming God who works through the hands of others and whose spirit helps to transform people and neighborhoods.

The sharp contrast between the three models of witnessing just presented is most clearly seen not in their size, financial backing, or scope of ministry. The most fundamental difference lies in the philosophy out of which each is motivated. While the first two are essentially about arguing for a case, the latter is about showing the way. While the first two are about following a script, the latter involves writing its own script. While the first two are about *doing* a ministry, the latter is about *being* in ministry.

I am convinced that the most effective discipleship occurs when we are engaged in *being* rather than *doing*. Energetic witness comes from being engaged in the task of loving others. When we are engaged in the task of loving others, we see the transforming power of God which changes us and equips us with good news to tell.

Today, Western culture is becoming self-obsessed. People are increasingly concerned with themselves, their own problems and difficulties, and ignoring all others. This is as true for nations as for individuals.

The more we look at ourselves as the center of the world, the greater their level of ill health. I am not suggesting that people should be unconcerned with "self," but rather that the self not be the central focus of life. A healthy respect for self is critical to well-being. However, more and more Western culture appears to be losing a wider focus on the world's problems and is seeing itself as a victim both personally and nationally.

The gospel principle of losing yourself to find yourself (Matthew 10:34 IV, 10:39 others; Mark 8:37 IV, 8:35 others; and Luke 9:24) should be a central part of personal and community life today. When we can surrender our own needs to the needs of others we are transformed, and then we truly have good news to tell. The Gospel of Matthew declares that we need to become like children. Douglas Hare suggests that the key to this passage is that we need to become like children, *without* status.

> Jesus' followers are here told that they must assume the status of a child, that is, they must join the lowest rank of stratified society. Those who are infected with the world's appetite for lording over others are here informed that this lust be completely surrendered.[2]

When we are engaged in loving others in the middle of their life situation, we are changed by the experience. It is then that we hear the gospel story told through the lives of the needy in a new way which is good news to tell.

Over and over again you hear of this principle finding expression in the lives of people who are overwhelmed by problems. Those involved in Camp Quality illustrate this. Camp Quality is a camping and support program for children with cancer. Started in Australia, it now operates around the world and has brought meaning into the lives of many thousands of volunteers who work with the children and their families.

I have heard many people say that despite having difficult personal pain or problems, when they engaged in the task of loving others, they were transformed. Energetic witness results from *be-*

ing, from loving, and from allowing ourselves to be transformed by human need as the power of God causes us to focus wholly on others.

Telling What You Know

While witnessing essentially concerns serving others, it also involves the important task of telling the story. More will be said about this later.

During 1994 and 1995 there was a great deal of public interest in the trial of O.J. Simpson in the United States. While the trial was being played out in the public media, it occupied many discussions in social circles, workplaces, and schoolrooms. Indeed, you only had to turn on the television or pick up a newspaper to find the opinion of an expert about the prosecuting lawyers, the "dream team" defense team, the judge, or the witnesses.

There was a great deal of conversation about the quality of witnesses over the course of the trial. Commentators regularly critiqued the reliability of certain witnesses during and after their period of testimony. Often the most pressing points of discussion were their credibility and the manner in which they conducted themselves. Some witnesses were considered more reputable than others. Some were referred to as professional witnesses. That is, they were people who regularly attended court, witnessing as experts in matters about which they are well informed. Some of those witnesses were considered by the commentators as poor witnesses, and others as great witnesses. From my observation, how they presented themselves was what determined the rating they received from the commentators.

Although very far from Christian witness, the experience of the courtroom tells us something about the value of witnessing. Those witnesses who spoke with pat answers, presented their own agenda, or used phrases that sounded like legal jargon were rated less highly by courtroom observers than those who spoke in simple language, listening to the questions and answering in a straightforward manner. That is also true for Christian witnessing.

Witnessing is most effective when it avoids the use of jargon, personal agendas, or pat answers and when it speaks "from the heart," telling what is known.

Transformed through Service

In 1993 my family and I spent a week in Missouri at the Jefferson City District reunion. My parents had traveled from Australia and joined us for the week. The summer of 1993 will be remembered by people in the U.S. Midwest for many years because of massive flooding. Heavy summer rains meant that the streams feeding the Missouri and Mississippi Rivers were full. These two majestic and powerful rivers overflowed, resulting in massive flooding and damage to the surrounding areas. For the tourist this was an awesome sight, but for the locals, it was a nightmare.

Near the middle of the reunion, we received word that a town not far from the campgrounds was being threatened by the Missouri River. Volunteers were sought to help build up the levees to keep the water from engulfing the town. The campers congregated in the auditorium where the need was discussed. More than half the camp volunteered to go. The rest of the adult campers remained at the grounds and cared for the many children.

Water bottles were filled, extra clothing was packed, and sun lotion was amply applied. We knew that a full day in the midwestern heat, coupled with high humidity, would mean that those working at the town might take a big personal toll.

I was one of those who left the campgrounds to help the local residents. There was an air of excitement as we began our adventure. When we arrived, we found the town already heavily sandbagged. Residents had built a wall more than three feet wide and nearly four feet high. The water was lapping over the top of this levee, even though normally it was at least a mile from the town. We joined many others already there, filling and passing sandbags and building up the walls. Why they are called sandbags, I don't know–after a while I was convinced that it wasn't sand we were putting in the bags, but cement! Although small in size, they were heavy.

Working a full day at the small town was an adventure. The local church provided lunch, a constant flow of cold drinks, and people regularly insisted we take breaks to rest. My father mentioned that he felt cared for as people would check to see how he was doing, making sure that the heat and hard work were not wearing him down. Over the course of the day we began to feel like a team. The goal was simple: to build up the wall and stop the river. We worked hard that day, and felt satisfied. At a moment's notice, we had responded to a call to help.

Later that evening we returned to the campgrounds to find a meal prepared and a camp full of happy people welcoming us and glad to see us. Many of those who stayed behind were weary from a day of working with the children. So we ate together, all of us glad to rest our bodies and be together. Later that night we worshiped.

It occurred to me that something special had happened that day. We became a united people, transformed into a community. It wasn't anything we could have planned that did this. Nor did any special activities make the difference. Rather, we became a united people by giving of ourselves for the sake of others. During the worship service that evening I was reminded of the people who rebuilt the walls of Jerusalem under Nehemiah's leadership. If Nehemiah had begun a campaign directly aimed at rebuilding the Jewish people into a united community, his efforts might not have had the effect they did. Instead, he called the people to service, and in the process a community was formed. That is exactly what we experienced on the banks of the Missouri River. The community we built came into being because of the selfless service everyone had given that day.

Through serving others, human life is transformed in a way that no emphasis on planning, skills workshops, or conferences ever could. At these moments we discover community as it is rarely experienced. And in the midst of this transforming experience, a new story is told. Not only is it the story of those alongside whom we are serving, but it is our story made new as we also are transformed. In such moments, our personal stories and witness are profoundly impacted and so is our collective experience.

This realization can have significant implications for congregations and groups who too often find themselves beset with low self-esteem and an inward-focused program, feeling stale, rundown, and tired. These feelings can be transformed as we give our hands and feet in the service of others, enfleshing our passionate witness.

Barriers to Energetic Witness

As we consider how our witness can be most effective, it is important to recognize that there are barriers that may stand in the way of the gospel being seen and heard by others.

1. Looking for technique. In this world of methodologies and "keys to successful whatever," it is hard to avoid the trap of looking for the "keys for successful witnessing," or of focusing on programs aimed at "how to win people to Christ without appearing to be a missionary." Such emphases not only reduce witnessing to technique learning but make many people think they should avoid witnessing because they lack the proper training or techniques, and so are ill-equipped.

2. Embarrassed or shy. Many of us are reluctant to witness because of embarrassment, believing we would be thought of as odd by friends if we introduced matters of faith into relationships. Culture has a lot to do with this. For example, in Australia, where I spent most of my growing-up years, to admit a commitment to Christianity and allegiance to a church is risky business. This is particularly true for young people. No, you wouldn't become a victim of crime, but you would be faced with ostracism and teasing. When people asked me my occupation (I am a full-time appointee minister), I would answer, "I am a minister for a church." The most frequent reply I received was: "A minister—what do you want to do that for?" The implication of the response was a doubting of religion's value and often a suggestion that I couldn't "get a proper job." Sometimes if I did not say I was a church minister but simply a minister, people would respond favorably, briefly thinking I was a minister in the government. Embarrassment and feelings of shyness about a faith commitment are frequent barriers to sharing an energetic witness.

3. Few opportunities. The final barrier is the lack of opportunities for witnessing. Most of us know lots of Christian people. We have friends and family members who belong to the church and socialize—sometimes exclusively—with them. Some say we are ingrown. Another way of looking at this is to observe that missionary and witnessing efforts in the past have proved effective, and so our family members, friends, and colleagues now share the same faith commitment as we do.

Nevertheless, living where many of our associates are Christian and/or already share membership in our faith community presents a challenge to us as we try to share an effective witness if our intent is to convert them to our point of view or bring them into our faith community. Rather, I suggest that this is not a problem if we simply share our witness without an underlying agenda. If our agenda is not conversion but witness, then sharing will have fewer strings attached to it and a greater degree of genuineness.

Removing Barriers

Being aware of the barriers to effective witnessing is important, but how do we go about removing those barriers and getting on with the task?

1. Work with the needy. When we are able to work with people in need, we are often more able to feel the Spirit of God at work in their lives and in our own. For most of its history, the church most often found itself working with people who were in need: the hopeless, the economically powerless, the uneducated, and struggling folk of the world. As a result of the power of the good news and the strength of the church community, as well as other social factors, many of those people are no longer found on the margins of society. In fact, many have become wealthy, educated, and significantly more powerful.

When we work with the kinds of people Jesus most often worked with, we often see lives change in a radical way. Christianity suddenly comes alive, and the Spirit of God appears to spontaneously bubble up in our congregations because of the joy of seeing new life in people's lives. Discipleship is most effectively lived out with those who are receptive to the good news: the poor, the powerless, the hopeless, the social and economic outcasts of our culture. When the gospel touches them, their lives are often changed forever.

The first time I ever went fishing with my wife, Tere, was on our honeymoon. We were vacationing in the Australian state of Tasmania. Trying to avoid Tasmanian devils, we decided to rent a small boat and try our hand at fishing–something that I enjoyed and tried to do as often as possible.

We had two lines, each with two hooks. Within a few minutes after throwing in the lines, the fish were biting. In fact, they were biting two fish to a line. It was my job to take the fish off the hooks and, because we were catching them to eat, to place them in the bucket. Tere was the catcher. It was her first time fishing, and within twenty minutes we had fourteen fish. So much for a quiet, romantic fishing expedition–the size of this catch was almost biblical! Even though we had more fish than we could handle, Tere was excited and wanted to go again.

In a sense, working with people in need is like that fishing trip. When we go to the place were we can help people and they want for us to work with them, often we are excited and want to keep at it. The gospel suddenly becomes something that we can see transforms people. The spirit of joy bubbles up and we too are transformed.

2. Find a small group in which to share your story. When I was young I shared in a youth ministry team called PROCLAIM. The name contained great significance and was an acronym for *P*ersons *R*eborn *O*f *C*hrist *L*iving *A*s *I*nspired *M*otivators! It was made up of twelve to fifteen youths between the ages of sixteen and twenty-five whose purpose was to bring revival and powerful witness to congregations. We met each week to learn together, share testimony, and plan for upcoming worship services. Under the leadership of experienced adults, and with the visible support of an evangelist couple, this group had a great influence on my life and on the lives of many others.

One of the things we would do was to hold each other accountable for having an effective witness. In fact, each week somebody was assigned to share a testimony. It needed to be recent, up-to-date, and punchy. After the testimony was shared, the group would critique it. That might sound a little harsh to many. Critiquing testimony is certainly something we don't do in public, although many do in the car on the way home from prayer meeting. But the reasons for the critique were specific. We wanted to avoid the preaching trap that people often fall into when witnessing. We also wanted the story to be up-to-date, and input from others helped us with that.

A colleague told me an instance of a young boy who, during a testimony service, summoned the courage to share. He stood on his seat, and when called on, started his testimony with the words, "Having been in the church forty years. . . ."

The most valuable thing about this group experience was hearing testimony from others, and being aware of the Spirit in others' lives and mine about which I could tell my story.

Being part of a group, whether it be a cell group, home fellowship, or family worship, helps to make us accountable for our own witness. It assists in having an up-to-date witness. It helps us be disciplined in looking for the action of God in our lives and the lives of others.

3. Serve others . . . and tell the story. I sometimes hear people say, "I don't need to tell people about Christ. I live by example, and they will see my actions and one day ask me what makes me different." While that may happen on occasion, I doubt that such events occur frequently. Further, it seems to me to be a bit presumptuous to think that another would look to us and say, "Wow, that person is special. What makes them so different." While many of us may think we are extraordinary, I frankly doubt that our actions are so different from many others that attention would be called to our saintliness!

We risk missing an opportunity to witness if we wait until others are impressed by our actions and ask why we are so special. It is far better to find opportunity to tell our story, not by drawing attention to ourselves, but by drawing attention to the grace of God which has been experienced in our life and the lives of our Christian friends. It is not because we are saintly that God is in relationship with us, but because we are broken. It is in our brokenness that we enter into relationship with God, and that is a message of hope to all our broken or searching friends.

Conclusion

James Kavanaugh speaks to the question of disclosure in the following poem:

Women gather
Free to chat of impotent husbands
and not quite forgotten lovers,
Sharing dreams with old and new friends
and confiding desperation,
Baring souls and unburdening hearts,
Then leave relaxed and laughing,
Promising to lunch again soon,
Freed from the pain of no one knowing.

Men gather
Free to boast of the money they've made
or will make soon—or the women,
Displaying how strong and controlled they are
and unafraid of competition,
Sharing triumphs and hiding themselves,

> Then leave with a handshake and "See you around,"
> Bleeding silently within themselves,
> Bearing the pain of no one knowing.[3]

Energetic witness requires that we engage in the lives of other people and expose something of our own sorrow and struggles. It requires authenticity, which means that we must immerse ourselves in others' lives, feeling their joys, struggles, and sorrows. Unlike an investment in an IRA or superannuation fund, this investment is made without the knowledge of what the return will be or even if there will be one. For our witness to be authentic, we must take the risk of entering into the experience of living with interdependence. While Kavanaugh speaks of women and men, those gender differences do not necessarily apply. Rather, his poem demonstrates the pain of living a life in isolated community. In the midst of the masses, people still wither from the pain of loneliness.

Energetic witness is not a technique or a method. In fact, it is not anything that can really be done. The call for energetic witness is found in the struggle to serve others. It is found when we serve others without expectation for reward or conversion. Our witness becomes energetic when we find ourselves in the service of other people, pointing to the hope found in the gospel.

Study Questions

1. The author makes a distinction between being and doing. What is the difference from your experience? When have you experienced people who try a technique as opposed to those who witness by being?
2. Review Mark 10:11–14 IV (10:13–16 others) and discuss the principle of becoming as little children in the task of witnessing.
3. What are the marks of an authentic witness?
4. The author points out several barriers to energetic witness. Discuss them, and identify other barriers that you or others might experience.
5. In what ways have you seen the church's role expressed in serving itself or serving other people? The author argues that service to people in need empowers our witness. How is this facilitated by your congregation's priorities? What could you do to engage in greater service?

6. The author says that "we miss an opportunity to witness if we wait until others are impressed by our actions and ask why we are so special." Do you agree with that? Should we tell others about the gospel, or should we wait until they ask about us?
7. James Kavanaugh presents a powerful image of isolation and alienation in his poem at the end of this chapter. Does this ring true to you? Are the gender differences he presents accurate from experience? How do these images relate to our witnessing?

Notes

1. James B. Nelson, *Body Theology* (Louisville, Kentucky: Westminster/John Knox Press, 1992), 123.
2. Douglas R. Hare, *Interpretation: A Bible Commentary for Teaching and Preaching Series* (Louisville, Kentucky: Westminster/John Knox Press, 1993), 208.
3. James Kavanaugh, reprinted in James B. Nelson, *The Intimate Connection: Male Sexuality, Masculine Spirituality* (Louisville, Kentucky: Westminster/John Knox Press, 1988), 47.

10

Sensitivity in Teaching and Learning

Trudi Mahi Gunderson

Which came first–the chicken or the egg? Who came first–the learner or the teacher? We are all learners and teachers. Teachers learn in their preparation to teach. Many professional teachers and professors know that dissemination of information is not teaching. The learners learn that memorization is not learning. In the next ten to thirty minutes it takes you to read this chapter, it is hoped you will experience the excitement of learning and teaching. We can be learner and teacher together. Ready? Begin!

The Learner-Teacher Team

As an English teacher in Japan, I discovered that life would be easier if I could count in Japanese. I observed mothers on trains and buses teaching their young children to count. Imagine my surprise when I learned there are at least ten different ways to count in Japanese. There are particular words for counting people, animals, cars, cylindrical items, flat items, books, houses, hard items, and soft items. If a shirt is folded, it is counted in one manner. When it is worn, a new counting word is used to identify the shirt. What a learning experience!

I enlisted the help of my Japanese language teacher. He decided we needed to be a team. During several class sessions we traveled through Tokyo counting different items in the city. The vendors would laugh politely when I used a counting word to identify pencils that should have been used for fish. However, because I was a foreigner or *gaijin* and making a sincere attempt to learn their language, the clerks in stores and markets would teach me the proper pronunciation and usage of words. We were a team!

Six months after my arrival in Seijo, Tokyo, Japan, one of the kindergarten teachers took maternity leave for about four months. It was difficult to find a full-time substitute teacher for the four month period. Mariko Saito, the principal, asked me to teach the oldest group, the Bluebirds. I was petrified! The students were to begin their Hiragana and Katakana writing, two of the Japanese phonetic alphabets. Mrs. Saito said she would help me, but I was lead teacher. I bought a children's writing book, memorized the key sentences and phrases I would need each day. The children knew I was not fluent in the Japanese language. They corrected me when it was necessary. They laughed at my mispronunciation of words. I once asked for a couple of noses instead of a couple of flowers. The children, whether consciously or not, wanted me to succeed. I wanted them to succeed. At the end of my substitution period the children knew their Katakana and Hiragana perfectly. So did I. We succeeded as a team.

One mother shared an important observation with me. Her daughter wanted me to be proficient in Katakana and Hiragana. The students felt they needed to be better than the teacher. I thought I was doing a great job. I could teach in any language—I must be a great teacher! I was made aware that the success of the class was based on a very simple principle: *Both teacher and student wanted the other to be successful.*

Every choir director wants his or her choir to sing well. The congregation listening to singers wants the performance to go well. Parents listening to their children play in their first music recital feel their stomachs tighten when their children's name and song are announced. They relax only after the successful, or slightly successful, rendition of "The Farmer's Song." Choir directors know where their choir struggles. Parents know when the E-natural should have been an E-flat. I always heard a sigh of relief from my parents when my recital number was finished. I also whispered a sigh of relief myself. I wanted my parents to be proud of me. I wanted to be proud of me.

My Auntie Bernice Ferreira was my first choir director. She let us know that if the altos did not sing their part well, the whole choir would be affected. I was an alto. Auntie Bernice would encourage each member to sing his or her best and listen to the next person. She would work with me individually if I was flat. I am sure she felt frustration. "It's a B-flat, not an A-natural!" she must have thought. However, not once did I hear resignation in her voice. She wanted me to succeed. I could not fail; the choir would not fail; the team would not fail!

The Kamehameha Schools in Honolulu, Hawaii, hold an annual song contest. The students know that one of their responsibilities as a Kamehameha student is their participation in the annual "Song Contest." The students compete by classes in an *a capella* contest. My brother, Aaron, and sister, Honey Bea, directed their respective classes. The student leaders work with a committee of teachers and peers in the selection and arrangement of Hawaiian songs. For three months before the contest, the classes practice at least once a week, pick the color for their class leis, and learn to present their songs to the public. When the "Song Contest" evening arrives, students have been told to get plenty of rest, dress neatly, not wear too much makeup, and arrive early to vocalize. Aaron and Honey Bea would express their frustration, happiness, anxiety, and hopes for their classmates. The students teach and learn from each other. Teamwork is a must. It has been thirty years since I sang in my last song contest, yet I can still feel the satisfaction of a job well done.

People who coach young people are also driven to succeed. The win-lose column has a degree of importance, but it is not the only gauge. Steady improvement in social skills, good health, enjoyment of the sport, communication skills, emotional development, understanding winning and losing, and parent participation are all elements in coaching young people.

As a Junior Olympics volleyball coach, I coach with others who are not only interested in winning, but feel there is a need for a whole-person approach to life. Recently I saw a T-shirt that said, "Second place is the first loser." I was enraged! What is learned by that? It goes against everything I believe as a teacher and a coach. There are many positive aspects of winning *and* losing. Coaches have the power to be catalysts in a teenager's understanding of winning and losing–on the field, on the court, in the classroom, and in the world.

God works with us in all aspects of our lives. God wants us to do the best we can. Even in failure we are able to succeed. Jesus lost his life on earth to overcome death. This earthly loss became a universal gain for humankind.

The Sensitive Teacher

Students are always better, more sensitive learners when the subject interests them. What does a teacher do when a student does not want to be in a class? Does the student learn? Does the teacher teach? Teaching students who do not want to learn presents a challenge for both student and teacher. Teachers, parents, grandparents, coaches, and facilitators find themselves in precarious situations when students feel they "have to" be in a class. A sensitive teacher is demanding, yet gentle; critical, yet constructive; competent, yet responsive.

A teacher's sensitivity begins with the will to teach. I knew I wanted to be a teacher when I was ten years old. The will to have a student learn is the will to teach. Sensitivity in teaching means being willing to extend oneself to students. It means showing vulnerability. It means the teacher learns while the students are learning. The will to teach means taking time to instruct and to follow through with students.

Nona Beamer, a storyteller, song writer, hula teacher, and Hawaiiana expert, has the will to teach. As a singer and hula dancer for our high school concert glee club, it was important for us to know the songs we danced and the importance of conveying that meaning to people who do not understand the Hawaiian language.

"Auntie Nona," as she is affectionately known by her students, demonstrated her will to teach her students. She would patiently repeat verses and phrases of ancient Hawaiian chants to her students. She studied the Hawaiian language, practiced with her students, reviewed their steps, and criticized with love. When her students failed in their feeling and performance of a particular song or dance, she would illustrate her point with a symbol of nature. "You want your hands to move softly as a cloud picking a flower," she would say. Her will and desire to teach were not draped with personal gain. I never observed her trying to push her opinions on others. She did demand discipline, tempered with consistency and concern. Her will to teach was guided by her desire to see her students know and feel connected with the music and their performance.

A teacher's sensitivity continues beyond the formal learning environment. The church school teacher who sends a note or birthday card to his students throughout the week is an example of Christian love and caring. I once sent postcards to my new junior high class students. It was a small gesture on my part. Little did I know what big rewards would be reaped. Teenagers, as well as adults, love to receive mail. It made them feel special.

At the closing service of a junior high camp in Missouri, the campers were asked to write the equivalent of New Year's resolutions. They placed the resolutions in a self-addressed stamped envelope. During the first week of school, the resolutions were mailed to the campers. Several campers remarked how they relived camp when they read and reread their resolutions. The counselors and teachers at camp had had a profound impact on the campers. Yes, they were teachers. Yes, they were sensitive beyond a formal classroom situation. And yes, they made a difference in the lives of the campers.

A teacher's sensitivity is dynamic. It grows as a teacher brings will, desire, integrity, and knowledge to the learning field. While many teachers take courses to improve their economic situation, there is also the drive to be a better teacher. The pool of knowledge in any given area increases dramatically in a relatively short time. Many of my "teacher friends" study to increase their competency and the competency of their students. They are not merely content with memorization of a subject. Their first concern is the student. Jesus was not concerned with the ability of people to memorize the Beatitudes. Jesus was more concerned with the ability and desire of people to live the Beatitudes.

As the "teacher sensitive" approach is used by teachers, parents, grandparents, extended family members, and friends, each person benefits. There is no age limit to being a sensitive teacher. As young and old alike learn from each other, a community's ability to mature is enhanced.

The Learner's Joy

Toddlers learning to walk laugh as they find they can use their legs to go from point A to point B. Young children laugh as they feel the wind on their faces when they are first able to maneuver a bicycle on their own. Teenagers shout when they pass the written test for a driving permit. Apprentices grin when they find they can fix the transmission of a car by themselves. College graduates both laugh and cry when they receive their degree and their first job. Parents are surprised to learn their daughter has been accepted to medical school. Grandparents delight in the accomplishments of both children and grandchildren.

Learning takes a lifetime. It also takes a moment. Learning involves understanding and living with the knowledge received and understood. With each new book I read, I find myself fascinated by my ignorance, yet grateful to have the opportunity to read and learn. Will I ever read all the books I want to read? Will I ever stop learning? I don't think learning ever stops.

When parents send their children out into the world as young adults, they hope their children are equipped with the "tools of life." They also hope their children will continue to learn and relearn the skills they need in life. Will they have a sense of responsibility? Will they have a passion for life? a job? maturity in decision making? ability to balance a checkbook?

After celebrating my high school graduation, my mother asked me if I had a ten-year plan. A ten-year plan? No. OK. My immediate thoughts were, "College, job, marriage, children, good health, etc., etc., etc." I sat down and made a list of the tasks I wanted to complete by my twenty-eighth birthday. My mother looked over my list and said, "Fulfill at least three-fourths of your list and you are on your way." On my way to what? Out of the ten items on my list (one task for each year, I reasoned), I completed nine. The tenth happened the following year.

Trudi's Ten-Year Plan

1. Obtain a teaching degree
2. Teach in Hawaii
3. Live in a foreign country
4. Travel around the world
5. Get married
6. Learn three foreign languages
7. Get my evangelists blessing
8. Write a story
9. Buy a brand new car
10. Learn about my family's history

While the list may not seem profound or grandiose, it did serve as a teaching guide for ten years of my life. As I accomplished each task, I crossed it off the list. I referred to the list occasionally and chuckled. Did my mother know she had taught me a valuable lesson? Did I know I was learning a valuable lesson? She did not force me to make the list. She never asked me which tasks were completed. She trusted and believed in my abilities.

With gentle guidance, my parents encouraged my siblings and me to formulate goals in our lives. I now think of my growing-up years as valuable. My parents demonstrated both sensitive teaching and learning with my brothers, sister, and me. They believed in our abilities but were realistic in their expectations. They offered criticism when needed although there were times we did not deem criticism necessary.

Showing respect facilitates learning. My parents gave us a sense of value and expectation in our lives. They were supported by my Grandpa Mahi, aunts, uncles, cousins, and our church family. The island-style extended family means that adults are addressed as "Auntie" or "Uncle." It would never occur to children in Hawaii to address adults by their first name. However, addressing adults by their first name in other social circles is considered appropriate. The kindergarten children in Japan showed respect for my position and addressed me as "Mahi Sensei"—"Teacher Mahi." As their teacher it was also important for me to show respect for their effort and learning. Again, the teacher-learner theory is reinforced.

Both teacher and learner gain from each other. The will, desire, and knowledge must be in both teacher and learner to be effective. It is not expected for teacher and learner to always be paragons. Rather, the joy of teaching and learning comes from the recognition that each side teaches and learns.

Study Questions

1. Why is the learner-teacher team important in a congregation?
2. How can the learner-teacher team enhance the life of the children in your congregation? the youth? the single parent? families? the congregational leadership team?
3. Describe Jesus as the "sensitive teacher." What can be learned from Jesus in this role?

4. In what ways can children, youth, and adults be joyful learners and sensitive teachers?
5. How can these suggestions be applied to the congregational setting?

11

Youth Ministry: A Circle of Friends

Michael A. Hoffman

Ministry to youth and children has an ancient history. Numerous examples of the importance of this ministry are evident in the scriptures. There was the caring Hebrew mother who placed her child in a reed basket and set it on a river, and the earthly parents who were given the opportunity to nurture and educate a baby born in a manger who would be called the Prince of Peace. Ministry to children and youth has had a major impact on not just our own personal lives but the history of Christianity.

Our own church history includes examples of ministry with children and youth that would go on to affect that very history. The founder of the church, Joseph Smith Jr., was a teenager when he first went into the grove and met the Divine. Joseph Smith III was nurtured by a widowed mother and friends of the family until the time he assumed the role of president of the Reorganization.

Personal Story

And so it goes–youth ministry today will shape the future of the church. My personal testimony is that youth ministry has had a dramatic affect on my life. If it were not for youth ministry I would not be writing this chapter, nor would I be serving as World Church youth minister. Let me explain.

My great-grandfather was converted to the Restoration more than a century ago, and I was raised in a good home. But during my growing-up years, my home had no connection with the RLDS

Church. During the 1960s, when I was a child, social pressures and work pressures kept my parents away from church. As I entered high school in the 1970s, the church was far from my mind as I began to explore life. Suffering from a poor-self image due to being overweight, I turned to alcohol. In the 1970s, there weren't any "Just Say No" campaigns or "alternative" parties. What I did find was that I could easily get alcohol. This, coupled with the fact that my parents went to a lake home almost every weekend, set up the perfect situation for me to become important to my high school peers. Holding parties at my house became my way to acceptance. While the neighbors sometimes called the police because of the noise or the cars parked in their yard, the police just closed us down for the night, never notifying my parents of such events. Remember, it was the 1970s, and alcohol was an acceptable form of entertainment to some degree.

As I entered college, it seemed natural for me to join a fraternity. Still searching for friends, and with no aversion to the consumption of alcohol, I reasoned that the monthly dues were a small price to pay to have such a large group of friends. But something unexpected happened during my time as a fraternity member. Part of the preparation for initiation was "Candle Week" during which those of us who were interested in joining had to tend a candle, taking turns carefully watching that it not go out. During our time at the candle, we were to read the Bible. The only Bible I had in the house was one imprinted on the front with my mother's maiden name and the strange words "Inspired Version." During Candle Week, one of my future brothers mentioned that I shouldn't use that Bible because it wasn't correct, corrupted by a would-be prophet. After being initiated in a beautiful Christian ritual, I continued my life as before, totally disregarding the message of the ceremony, as did every other brother I knew.

But something unforeseen was stirring on my college campus. The dean of students, who at that time was a member of the RLDS Church, gave my name to a group of students trying to form a Liahona Fellowship. I guess that I had indicated on my entrance papers that RLDS was my religious preference although, as I look back on that time, it seems odd that I would have done so because I had little or no connection with the church. As this group tried to organize they contacted me. "Ha!" I thought. At that point in my life I had finally found what I thought was the answer to my self-esteem problem: I had become a "BMOC," big man on campus. I was president of the largest, most active fraternity on campus and editor of the college yearbook. I was not only on the student senate but had announced my intention to run for Student Government Association president. "What? Me need this disorganized little band of people? Ha!" I told them no way was I interested in the Liahona Fellowship!

But one particular young woman just wouldn't give up on me. She kept talking to me at every opportunity. She even joined the yearbook staff and kept after me as we worked together.

After a year of developing a friendship, she again invited me to a church activity. This time it was a retreat. I knew from my fraternity experience what retreats were, or at least I thought I did. But little did I realize what changes attending this event would bring to my life.

In the ensuing months, I became friends with all the members of the little Liahona group, including a young woman who would later become my wife. Slowly I began to sense the Holy Spirit working in my life. Many changes took place, the most significant of which was my baptism and confirmation in April 1980. Later that year, I decided to resign from my fraternity. It had become a lifestyle I no longer could support, even though there were a handful of my fraternity brothers who also developed a relationship with Christ that year and began to attend different churches. At one point we even held Bible study in the fraternity house living room.

The reason I have shared this story with you is to illustrate that my church membership and relationship with Jesus Christ came about because a young disciple did not give up on me. She became my friend and introduced me to people, all of whom also became good friends. After these friendships had become solid, this young woman asked if I wanted to be baptized. I said yes, because in this circle of good friends I had seen the light of Christ and had felt the call of community.

Challenges for Today's Youth

Toward the end of his earthly ministry, Jesus called the disciples "friend" because they knew him, and knew his vision. Unlike the relationship between a master and slaves, in which the slaves have no idea what the master is doing, Jesus called them friends.

As the church nears the last few years of the twentieth century, our youth are faced with new challenges that most adults never faced as they grew up. This will require new models of youth ministry if the church is to continue to reach future generations. We must continue to translate the gospel into the language, symbols, and methods that will reach young people with the call of Christ. When people are hungry, do you give them bread or a stone? In the same manner, when young people seek the gospel should we give them books with outdated language and illustrate sermons with images that have nothing to do with their lives?

Any new models of ministry must take into account the time commitment servant ministers must make in order to provide this ministry. Today the relationships young people have are under a great deal of stress. Relationships with parents—whether they have one or two in the home where they live—are often negatively affected by the large time commitment necessary to financially support the family. Friendships between youth are also affected by the same circumstance. Many children and youth live with only one parent, who at times must be both mother and father. So what shall we do?

We must build friendships with youth, and they with us. And "us" is a focal point. Unless congregations have the assets to allow them to hire full-time youth ministers, most will need to develop a team who can bring ministry to children and youth. For teens this must include those youth who are willing and able to bring ministry to their peers. Time is the new method of measuring worth.

If you value someone, you will spend time with them. I once heard a new definition of a friend: someone with whom you are willing to waste time. How profound! Not just spending productive time with them, but being willing to *waste* time with them. This may be a contemporary definition of unconditional love.

The Gospel and Youth

To successfully translate the gospel into the language of today's children and youth, we must become partners with them. Many, but not all, of our children have incredible access to information about the gospel. They can study scripture from CDs and send communications to friends around the world through e-mail on the Internet. They can listen to music or messages everywhere they go, any time they want. We must help them understand which messages represent the "Good News" and which do not. When we tell stories and illustrate the principles of the gospel, we must tie them to the life experiences of youth such as situations at school, dating, and family relations. Learning experiences must become active, concrete examples of the gospel in real life, not merely stories of other people. Youth want to get their hands dirty, get directly involved, and sense from others that they've had an impact on their lives.

In many cases the way we "do church" must change as well if we wish to actively involve youth in the life of the community of Christ. I'm not sure that I can even project what methods will need to be used in the future. Certainly approaches to youth ministry will vary considerably from congregation to congregation. In some areas youth might be linked by computer; in others the use of video, CDs, etc., could be helpful. Classes might be interactive between youth in isolated congregations with those located in urban areas or perhaps between countries, if not continents.

However, regardless of the situation, every person needs a close circle of friends through which to receive love, affirmation, and touch. It will not be enough to communicate through media. While information may be shared in this way, the love of Jesus Christ is better communicated personally rather than, for example, by fax where no human touch occurs.

Worship

As we look at ways to effectively minister to youth, we must consider the worship life of the congregation. Think for a moment about times when you have observed young people worshiping. My mind flashes back to rock concerts. No, the purpose of such events is not to worship God, but the fervor of youth at these concerts closely matches the enthusiasm we hope they will display in the worship of God. They pay for seats (offering?) and stand up most of the time listening to music and singing with it. Usually they have gone with a group of their friends. They sing, shout, clap, all elements of exuberant worship today. They buy souvenirs to remind them of the experience. They even purchase bulletins (whoops, programs!).

In Tony Campolo's book, *The Kingdom of God Is a Party*,[1] this youth minister from Philadelphia explains that to convey the message of the kingdom of God to today's youth we need new, fresh approaches to reach them. He draws the parallel between the kingdom and the term "party." When I first heard this idea, I must admit it concerned me. I remember parties, like those in high school and with my fraternity, that could never be seen as a model for the worship of God. But Tony Campolo is not talking about this type of party. Instead, he is describing the spirit of joy that is resident in those who come to a birthday party. At such times we cherish our friends, have fun, and celebrate life as a gift from God. A birthday party is not a time to be somber, sad, and straight-faced. Neither is it a time to recite meaningless verbiage.

Caring and Support

As Jesus is our model, we are called to a youth ministry that provides joy, healing, caring, and blessing. These can come in many ways, through prayer, counseling, and the ministry of presence during times of crisis or transition in life.

Adolescence is a time of major transition as youth experience such things as the onset of raging hormones, graduations, dating, and learning to drive. As they experience these new experiences, Christians are called to care by being available and vulnerable, reflectively listening, and sharing their concerns.

Vision

At this time of transition, many youth also struggle with their life's direction. The ministry of vision becomes important as they go through these years. This involves helping them develop a vision for their own lives; affirming our vision for them; encouraging them with truthful, positive comments; and including them in our lives, our congregations, and our efforts at ministry.

Teaching/Learning

The church is called to provide opportunities for youth to learn. Sometimes this involves teaching; or it may mean just getting out of their way. A precursor to helping others learn is to know who they are, which requires a commitment of time. Learning takes place in many ways, in many places, and at many different times. Christian education is not just something that happens for one hour on Sunday morning. It happens at home, at school, at parks, in neighborhoods, in hospitals–you name it. Youth ministers should be with youth at those special times that have come to be called teachable moments.

Communities of Joy

Exciting youth ministry must embrace the three elements of the Communities of Joy emphasis: vision, mission, and celebration.

What is your vision of youth ministry? Regardless of where you are, you must consider a vision for youth ministry. Many times we are limited in our success by our vision. On occasion I encounter someone who says, "We only have two or three children/youth in our congregation." If you are such a person, I say to you, "Look around!" Your vision is narrow. There are countless children and youth who are unchurched. Perhaps you've limited your vision to "children and youth of active families" or "children and youth of book membership." Why not consider children and youth who do not yet have a relationship with Jesus Christ in your county/city/town/neighborhood/school/family/community?

Next, consider your mission. If you've got an active group already, regardless of size, seek input from the youth and develop your own mission statement. Various tools for doing this are available from World Headquarters and Herald House. Youth are an important part of the church's mission and should not have to wait until they are adults to be actively involved in sharing the gospel and building the kingdom. It is vital for youth to see their mission as closely related to the mission of the congregation.

Finally, youth ministry must celebrate life as a gift from God. Celebrate relationships, birthdays, friendships, witnessing, good feelings of helping others, and stories.

One of my fondest personal memories of celebration concerns a day I spent working with Habitat for Humanity. Our youth group went out to help with a minor painting and landscaping project. My job was to place old railroad ties as edging along a driveway and secure them by hammering rebars through pre-drilled holes and into the ground. On the first piece, I hammered for a long, long time before I realized it had hit the edge of the cement driveway. When I took this piece of rebar out of the railroad tie, it was curled and bent. I kept that piece of metal for weeks as evidence of the intensity with which I had worked. I celebrated the work of the youth group the next Sunday by showing the congregation my fabulously curled piece of rebar.

The essence of exciting youth ministry in the church is attitude. Attitude is the way you position yourself as you consider life. Are you optimistic? Are you helpful? Or are you trapped by baggage from the past, which holds you down and hinders you from ministering to the youth and children of your congregation?

Study Questions

1. Through what circle of friends were you introduced to the church? What impact did your circle of friends have on you regarding your response to the church when you were younger?
2. How do you spend your time? How does it indicate those things of value?
3. What are some ways you can "translate" the gospel into language and symbols for today's youth? What are some methods for reaching children and youth that have developed just in the last few years?
4. Explain how learning experiences become active, using concrete examples.
5. What methods can be included in congregational worship that will include input and experiences for children and youth, as well as adults? What are the differences between adult worship and youth worship?
6. How can you offer support to adolescent youth, who are facing transitions in this period of life?
7. What is your vision for your youth ministry? What would the ideal youth ministry look like? In what ways can that vision be expanded?
8. What is the mission of your youth ministry? What are the goals and objectives?

9. How do you celebrate youth ministry? In what ways does your celebration lift up children and youth? How is the congregation involved? How does this affect worship?

Notes

1. Tony Campolo, *The Kingdom of God Is a Party* (Dallas, Texas: Word Publishing, 1990).

12

As a Little Child

Martha J. Pack

Children have a unique ministry to share. Not only are we to learn from them and follow their lead, but also we have the awesome responsibility to be an example as well. We need to involve them and consider them to be an integral part of our communities of Christ today, or they may not choose to be a part of the church tomorrow. If we intentionally help children know how very much God loves them, that they have ministry to give, and provide them opportunities to offer that ministry, it is much more likely they will choose to be a part of tomorrow's community of Christ .

Love is the key to guiding children to God.

> Love is patient and kind; it is not jealous, or conceited, or proud; love is not ill-mannered, or selfish, or irritable; love does not keep a record of wrongs; love is not happy with evil, but is happy with the truth. Love never gives up; and its faith, hope, and patience never fail.
>
> —I Corinthians 13:4–7, Today's English Version

As parents and extended family of the congregation, we can be images of God's love to all of God's people and especially to children. Our responses to the children, whether they are behaving appropriately or not, give them their first impression of what our heavenly Parent is like. Our behavior toward and words about others do not go unnoticed. Children look at adults as models of what God is like. Because they are so close to their children, parents carry a special responsibility to be sure their children feel loved and grow up sensing the love of God around them.

A young father himself, Thom Hunter tells of the pain he felt when he discovered that in the many pages of his own father's diaries Thom's name was never mentioned. As a consequence, Thom was impressed to make it clear to his own five children how much they mean to him. He wants it to be clear to them that they are more than just a small measure in his life. He does this because he knows from experience that children doubt their parents' love sometimes, no matter how obvious the parents may try to make that love appear.

Henri J. M. Nouwen tells of a time when, as a small child, he asked his parents "Do you love me?" so often it became a source of irritation. Yet, even so, he still never felt fully satisfied with their response.[1]

Do our children know we love them? Most of us would answer emphatically, "Yes! Of course they do!" However, no matter what we say, children will test our loving faithfulness and in many ways continually try to find out not only *if* we love them but *how much* we love them. For children, it is never a closed issue. They constantly wonder, "Do you love me now? Do you love me more than. . . ?"

When my son, Danny, was in second grade, his music teacher, Jesse Weldon, had a program that demonstrated what the children had learned. Clearly Danny had a musical understanding far greater than the other children, and Jesse found ways to let him demonstrate his talent. I was very proud of him. In fact, during the program I resolved to begin music lessons with him immediately. It was something I had put off because I remembered how, as a child, I had not particularly enjoyed having to practice. But with his obvious propensity for music, I realized that I could not ignore my responsibility to help his giftedness grow.

I left the music program without saying a single word to Danny about his performance that day. My parents had always done similarly to me and I came to understand their reasoning was that it was not proper to brag about oneself. After all, I thought, don't the scriptures tell us to be humble?

When Danny came home from school that day, he brought a note he had made for me. The simple message in that note made an indelible impression on me. It said: "Dear Mother, I love you. Do you love me?" Clearly, he did not know. I sat down with him immediately and tried to tell him, but I could see in his eyes I was getting nowhere. My actions had said it all. I remembered that when I was a child I, too, had often wondered if my parents loved me. I knew then I needed to find ways to help Danny understand that I did love him and how much I loved him.

Children have a sense of discernment that serves them well in infancy as they are growing and developing. They know whether or not we are sincere. We have to exhibit an attitude of caring concern matched by consistency in our actions or they will know it is just rhetoric.

Children wonder, "Do you love me, Dad, enough that it is as important to you to spend an hour with me every week like you spend with your favorite TV program?" We think that because we go to work every day, pay our bills, keep our house clean, and our lawn mowed that we are doing all these things for our children. But wouldn't we do all these things even if we had no children? Children already have this figured out. They want to know what else we are going to do to persuade them that we love them. They want proof.

This is such an important issue that Christ asks us the same question as asked of Simon: "Simon, son of Jonas, lovest thou me more than these? . . . Simon, son of Jonas, lovest thou me?" (John 21:15–16). Simon's response was as ours today: "Yea, Lord; thou knowest that I love thee." To which Christ's response of "Feed my sheep" meant, "Prove it."

As the extended family and community of Christ we can say to each other, "Of course we love our children. We can prove it! We have church school, kids' church, children's choir, and vacation church school." However, when we look at some of the ways our children struggle with everyday choices revolving around issues of self-worth, autonomy, and love, we often have to acknowledge that evidently our children are not convinced of our unconditional love for them or that they are truly and unconditionally loved by God.

A few years ago an extensive survey was conducted to discover how children identify and define love. Two things were consistently mentioned: affectionate touch and time spent with them. Children thrive on hugging, holding, and time spent in listening, playing, and doing things together. The study went on to point out that if children do not feel loved, they cannot accept and love themselves or others.[2]

Once we have established a loving relationship with our children, they will feel free to be themselves and share their unique gifts in loving, serving ways.

Jesus advised, "Whosoever will not receive the kingdom of God as a little child, shall in no wise enter therein" (Luke 18:17). Thus children have something to teach us. They have ministry to give. Jesus calls us to learn to be like children, not to teach children to be like us. Their nature as givers of free, unconditional love must become our nature. If we want children to be like us, we have to first become like them.

Children can bring ministry no matter what age they are. Their capacity for compassion is inspiring. One of the boys in the choir, Kyle, at only ten years of age, suggested to the other boys that they all shave their heads. They didn't want Ian, who was undergoing chemotherapy, to feel out of place when they sang on Sunday morning. Because of their love for their friend, they responded freely to the Spirit of Christ within themselves and set an example we would find difficult to follow.

One Sunday during my congregation's "Kid's Church," I didn't have any specific responsibility; I was helping by just being there. We had a few minutes while we were waiting for the next activity to be set up. While the children were waiting quietly, I pulled out one of those big packs of gum containing eighteen sticks. Shelby and Kayla went around the room quietly tearing each stick in half and giving each child a piece of gum. Although I did not count the pieces of gum, I was comfortable that there would be enough for everyone to have half a piece. However, it came down to Shelby having one piece left and there were three children who did not yet have gum. Quickly I began to think about how I might resolve this. I thought about giving the remaining children a peppermint lifesaver from the roll in my purse, but I decided to see how they would work out the problem.

Rachael, who did not come to church very often, was only there because her grandmother had brought her. I asked her if she would like to share. Her response was emphatic, brief, and normal for a five-year-old, "No!" To emphasize the point, she quickly unwrapped her piece and popped it into her mouth.

Shelby held the last half piece in her hand and looked at Joshua who was the other child who did not yet have gum. She turned to me and said, "I'll share." She then tried to tear the half piece equally but ended up with one very small piece and a much larger piece. She looked at them both and couldn't quite decide what to do, but finally offered Joshua the smaller piece. I felt blessed as I noticed the beautiful spirit Joshua exhibited. He was delighted to have even that small piece.

However, as Joshua's hand reached out to receive the small piece and before his fingers met Shelby's, she switched hands and gave him the larger piece. Shelby and Joshua's actions taught me powerful lessons about love, giving, sharing, compassion, empathy, appreciation, and stewardship.

The prophet Isaiah said, "a little child shall lead them" (Isaiah 11:6). If we are willing to be led, we will discover that "we are never too old to learn and children are never too young to teach."[3]

The week before my daughter Sue's baptism was hectic. We had attended our stake's reunion. On the day we returned, we went to a family reunion, and on the way home had a car accident. Thankfully, no one was injured, but the confusion caused by the accident just made the day even more hectic. The next morning as we were getting ready for church, I realized I had not given any thought whatsoever to what Sue would wear while being baptized. I had visions of the other little girls in pristine white lacy dresses and I regretted my oversight. The only thing Sue had that was white was an angel costume I had made for her the previous Christmas. Being a practical person, I had made it out of flannel and Sue wore it sometimes as a nightgown. Although it was in a heap in a corner of the closet, it appeared to be clean so we decided it would be fine. I was thankful that Sue really did not care what she did or did not have to wear that day.

The minister, Gordon Andes, brought the challenge and used an object lesson. He had a shoe box into which he placed a jar of dirty water and then raised up a jar of clear water. It was quite impressive.

When the time came for the candidates to change into their garments I noticed Sue had evidently worn the nightgown while drinking cocoa. Sure enough, there were stains on the gown. I debated telling Sue to try to hold the folds of the flannel so that it wouldn't show while she was getting into the font, but I didn't want her to feel bad about what she was wearing and so I kept quiet.

When Sue came out of the font, I helped her change into dry clothes. As I was wringing out the gown, I noticed that the cocoa stains were gone. I couldn't believe it. I looked again. There were no cocoa stains.

Sue was oblivious to all of this going on in my mind. Her heart was truly in the right place as she accepted the Lord into her life and accepted the responsibility of that action. She appeared perfectly content in the knowledge that God cared about her. She didn't even notice what was on her body.

But I thought of what a testimony this was, and when the time appeared to be appropriate, I would share this incident with Sue. But just to be sure, I looked really hard once more. Just as I thought. The cocoa stains were really there after all: I have this tendency to look for what is wrong, and when I keep looking hard enough, I find it. It's an adult "thing" that children don't do.

Stephen Covey[4] would no doubt remind us that children operate most of the time in Quadrant 2–in other words, whatever they are doing is important to them, but they do not innately view it as an emergency. They are constantly (not deliberately, but naturally) working on their relationships, opportunities, and recreational activities, and they usually view others as people of equal value. So we could paraphrase the scripture in Luke to say, "Whosoever will not operate in Quadrant 2 as a little child, shall not have the highest effectiveness in the kingdom of God." Because it is our desire to be *effective,* we need to pay attention to the lessons we can learn from our children.

Nathan's face glowed with a knowing smile as he sat perched on the edge of his seat so his short legs could swing freely. He looked around the room acknowledging the familiar surroundings of the church sanctuary. When his eyes met mine, he pointed. I understood this to mean that he wanted to come sit with me. I smiled back and nodded my head ever so slightly, enough for Nathan to know I welcomed his visit. We found quiet things to explore in my purse and after a time, he returned to his parents.

The following week Nathan again visited me. And even though the week after that his family happened to sit farther away, he waved to me several times. Nathan was about the business of serving God because, without fully understanding why, Nathan's visits brought quiet joy to my heart. He didn't know it, but his openness and love reminded me how comfortable children are with me and I with them. I had recently transferred into the congregation and had been wondering where I should give my service. Because of Nathan's ministry, I understood that, for the present, I needed to be with children because I have a lot more to learn from them.

Children have an uncanny ability to discover and deliver the truth, and we're often caught off guard by their insight, imagination, and truth-piercing humor.[5] Sometimes they help us clarify incidents in our own minds as we attempt to share the beautiful stories of Christ, such as when Eli pointed to the baby Jesus in the manger and said, "There's Wayne." When his mother asked why he thought the baby's name was Wayne, he began to sing, "A Wayne in a manger."

When an opportunity was provided for the children to draw a picture about the Christmas story, Jennie drew an airplane with a pilot and three passengers. Her explanation was that Mary, Joseph, and the baby were on a flight to Egypt with Pontius as the pilot.

Children also have pure hearts that tend to see only the good in others as they respond to ministry being offered them. Christina was excited as her family drove home from church. "I saw Jesus today at church, Momma!" Her mother couldn't believe it, but asked, "When was that?" "You saw him too, Momma. Remember? He said goodbye to us at the door." Tina's mother did remember that Brother Graham, a kind and gentle minister, had been at the church door when they left that day. Tina had seen Christ in his manner—something her mother had not noticed.

Of utmost importance to the spiritual development of children—and for the life of the congregation—is the need for children to be involved in congregational worship. Opportunities need to be provided for them to share their ministry, as well as for them to receive ministry from others.

> The truth is we must welcome children into worship not just because they need to be there (which they most certainly do) but because without them, we cannot properly hear the gospel. . . . Going to church with children may be one of the most important things which you can do in the service of your Lord and for the increase of his kingdom.[6]

Yet many children do not see the church sanctuary until they reach an age when they are too old for the nursery. Jesus said, "Inasmuch as ye have done it unto one of the least of these my brethren, ye have done it unto me" (Matthew 25:41 IV). We cannot imagine keeping Jesus as a child from seeing the inside of the sanctuary.

Children need to feel a sense of belonging with adults and in the "main" sanctuary. Children do not go to church just to learn, but to feel—feelings of community, joy, welcome, reverence, awe, importance, and of occasion. They want to feel needed and missed if they are absent. They want to feel they are valued participants in the community and share a full sense of belonging. Each child needs to feel a sense of calling—a belief that he or she is called for just "such a time as this" (Esther 4:14). It is tempting for children to think that belonging and living as part of God's kingdom is a very adult thing to do. All too often, children see only adults participating in worship.

Jesus was genuinely open to children, even when the disciples wanted to turn them away. Jesus didn't send them to the olive grove on the next hill over for their own lessons. We should not feel that children are interrupting when we help guide their young eyes across the page, listen to their questions, or point out where we are in the bulletin. Jesus said, "Whoever welcomes a little child like this in my name welcomes me" (Matthew 18:5 New International Version).

At confirmation the Holy Spirit is "officially" bestowed. Even so, children are born spiritually sensitive, and recent child development research confirms that in the first five years of life a child decides the answers to these important questions:

- Who am I?
- To whom do I belong?
- In what environments do I feel comfortable?[7]

Certainly, we want one of those comfortable environments to be the community of Christ family.

When Caryn, a charming four-year-old, was asked what she learned at church, she answered, "Nothin'—'cause all we did was sit." Although it is clear what Caryn meant by "nothin'," there is insight in her words of wisdom. If our main concern while worshiping is to be quiet and still, we may give the impression that worship is a physical posture more than communion with God or that church is a building instead of a people. Extraordinary comprehension for such a young mind.

It is important that children have happy experiences at church that will lay a foundation for fellowship and imprint on them a familiar sense of identity with the worshiping community so that it becomes a part of them. When the winds of uncertainty blow and they question who they are, the unconscious mind will affirm, "You are a child of God."

I once saw a Dennis the Menace cartoon in which Dennis runs to his mother's arms and with tears in his eyes says, "I HAD to come home. I need somebody to be on MY side!" We want our children to feel that way about God—that God is always ready to hold them tight and be on their side.

When we contemplate the total picture of our community of Christ, we cannot help but think about our children and how they impact us with their ministry. Not only do they bestow joy on us through their ministry of presence, but their point of view offers an original perspective and their insights often cause us to dig deeper.

In our community of Christ family, we are all responsible for all the children. Even though they are not biologically ours, they are spiritually, emotionally, and physically ours. When they entered the congregational family, they forever changed it. The family will never be the same.

We are called into covenant relationships in community with all God's children. "As each one has received a special gift, employ it in serving one another, as good stewards of the manifold grace of God" (I Peter 4:10, New American Standard Bible). Our children have as much ministry to give us as we have to give them.

Members of each community will determine how to go about facilitating worship with and for children. Kids' church or junior church can be an appropriate vehicle, but it is also important that children be included in the corporate worship of the whole community, not just from time to time, but regularly.

The community of Christ will benefit from the ministry of children as it welcomes them into its arms and "counts them all joy."

Questions for Consideration

1. What do you honestly think is the most important thing that happens on Sunday at church?
2. Consider the scripture "Children are a gift from the Lord" (Psalm 127:3 Good News Bible). How do you feel when a child near you begins to get noisy during the service? Is it OK for children to do quiet things (like doodling) during the worship service?

3. How do you express love for the children in your congregation? Try to express what you feel when you think about a child you truly love. Do earthly words seem finite and inadequate?
4. Are you willing to sacrifice something (for example, being able to concentrate on or hear the service) for a child's spiritual development?
5. Would you personally be willing to form a faith relationship (friendship) with a child in your congregation?
6. Should the children in your congregation go to junior church every Sunday? Is it appropriate to have one at all?
7. What are some ways that could enable children to share their ministry with your congregation during your worship services? Is it possible to have worship services that will be meaningful and include people of all ages?

Notes

1. Henri J. M. Nouwen, *Here and Now: Living in the Spirit*, (New York: Crossroads, 1994).
2. Don and Katie Fortune, *Discover Your Children's Gifts: A Parent's Handbook to Recognize and Develop Your Children's God-Given Gifts* (Grand Rapids, Michigan: Chosen Books, 1989), 187.
3. H. Jackson Brown Jr., *Wit and Wisdom from the Peanut Butter Gang: A Collection of Wise Words from Young Hearts* (Nashville, Tennessee: Rutledge Hill Press, 1994).
4. Stephen R. Covey, *The Seven Habits of Highly Effective People* (New York: A Fireside Book, Published by Simon & Schuster, 1989).
5. H. Jackson Brown Jr., *Wit and Wisdom.*
6. Stan Stewart with Pauline Stewart and Richard Green, *Going to Church with Children* (Melbourne, Australia: The Joint Board of Christian Education, 1987), 5, 7.
7. Ibid., 95.

Other Suggested Readings

Halverson, Delia. *Introducing Children to God, Jesus, the Bible, Prayer, Church.* Nashville, Tennessee: Abingdon Press, 1993.

Hunter, Thom. *Those Not-So-Still Small Voices: God Says the Most Amazing Things Through Your Kids.* Colorado Springs, Colorado: NavPress, 1993.

Waldrop, C. Sybil. *Guiding Your Child toward God.* Nashville, Tennessee: Broadman Presss, 1985.

13

Community of Supportive Families

Karen F. Freberg and Gail E. Mengel

It is appropriate that we write this chapter together. We are sisters who, along with our brother, were raised by parents in a home where our mother had lived since she was twelve years old. We attended the congregation where our great-grandparents, great-aunts and uncles, grandparents, aunts, uncles, and cousins attended. Our roots were deep and familiar, our relationships were strong and committed, and we were embraced by a supportive and loving community.

However, life changed dramatically for us as adults. We found ourselves living thousands of miles away from one another, and our relationship had to be sustained by letters, phone calls, and holiday visits. Our congregations were valued places for worship and for support. We found love in communities of Saints that responded as extended families. As young adults we participated in congregations with families who cared for one another and held each other up. It seems so natural to live in a family with those we love. And yet, statistics and stories confirm the struggles and complications that disrupt and often divide us.

Jesus gave no explicit instructions for family life. However, he did give guidelines that have spanned the centuries and transcended differences.

" 'You shall love the Lord your God with all your heart, and with all your soul, and with all your mind.' This is the greatest and first commandment. And the second is like it: 'You shall love your neighbor as yourself.' " (Matthew 22:37–39 NRSV).

In giving instruction to a rich young man, Jesus was more explicit in regard to the older generation and to peers. "Honor your father and mother; also, You shall love your neighbor as yourself." (Matthew 19:19 NRSV).

He was equally clear about relationships with the youngest generation. "Then little children were being brought to him in order that he might lay his hands on them and pray. The disciples spoke sternly to those who brought them; but Jesus said, 'Let the little children come to me, and do not stop them; for it is to such as these that the kingdom of heaven belongs.' " (Matthew 19:13–15 NRSV).

Jesus brought us all into the family of God. "And he replied, 'Who are my mother and my brothers?' And looking at those who sat around him, he said, 'Here are my mother and my brothers! Whoever does the will of God is my brother and sister and mother.' " (Mark 3:33–35 NRSV).

Then Jesus offered a prescription for relationships in his family: "This is my commandment, that you love one another as I have loved you." He expanded the message and taught us about unconditional love. "And the king will answer them, 'Truly I tell you, just as you did it to one of the least of these who are members of my family, you did it to me.' " (Matthew 25:40 NRSV).

From the Gospels we learn that Jesus had contact with people of all life stages and with much diversity in family situations. Jesus himself established a kind of alternative family when he chose the twelve disciples. They traveled with him, ate with him, learned his teachings, and practiced ministry. Jesus provided us with many examples of living in supportive relationships which remain our best models for today. Christianity is about relationship.

> So why is . . . [a sense of community and unconditional love/support] . . . needed within families? Perhaps because the level of emotion and caring is so deep. Those whom we love so much are also the subject of our dreams and the objects of our frustration, anger and disappointment. For all the times in which we reach out to nurture and support the ones we love, there are also times of crisis and stress when we do not know how to respond to, or how to include, the other members of our family.[1]

At the heart of our creative family life is an awareness of the power beyond human definition which enables us not only to be ourselves but to be in relationship to one another."[2]

We are called to participate as partners, not only for ourselves, but for the empowerment of all members of the family of God. This is easier when we bring to the congregation our experiences that prepared us for relational living–love, nurture, protection, and time and space to grow as an individual.

While every generation has faced changes that challenge traditions, we have been impacted by technological, environmental, and social changes which have influenced life at our foundation. For several decades we have been a transient society. Families don't remain in the same city or congregation for a lifetime. Therefore, relationships no longer benefit from years in a supportive community. We are challenged as never before. To consider communities of joy and supportive families, we must examine some critical realities and look for ways to respond that will influence that vision and create hope within the people.

Critical Realities

We hear a lot these days about "family." We are inundated with information about everything from family restaurants to family worship services, family TV to family vacation spots, family support groups to family counseling, family abuse to family health, family break-up to family healing.

Family life and family structure have changed more in recent years than ever before in history. Women in the work force, the rapid increase of the number of families in poverty, divorce and blended families, sexual activity at earlier and earlier ages, increased stress and unresolved anger, the accelerating development of technology, and chemical addiction are among the variety of causes that are contributing to the changing reality and challenge of families. This is accompanied by a nostalgic longing for a time when families were stronger, more secure and predictable, even as some predict the death of the family we struggle now to know and understand.

Our congregations include a variety of families who experience all these and more vivid current realities. Therefore stress, lack of trust, distance, individuality, brokenness, lack of time and energy, and commitment to many activities and causes challenge the time-honored precepts of unity, dedication, joy, good news, hope, wholeness, and common purpose. The congregation is confronted with a loss of a sense of community, of responsibility, and of legacy. We are a generation of individual loners struggling in our individual lives, in our families, and then in our congregations.

In most ministries and programs, the congregation has become the carrier, comforter, and upholder of families formed by society and culture. This, of course, is our mission, but not our sole calling. We need to sound the alarm for discussion, for an encounter with society–its values and norms. Congregations need to be proactive in creating environments, standing for Christlike virtues, and offering ministries that value individuals and families. In the midst of all that is, we are called to discover that which brings wholeness and hope.

These are critical realities and challenges. How do congregations offer ministries that speak to the hearts and minds of families–all ages? How do congregations blend a variety of families and celebrate the diversity? How do congregations become "family" and build a companion life of trust, confidence, sharing, and caring?

Changing Image

Consider how your life has changed in the last decade or two. Think about the toys you played with as a child, compared with "toys" today. Children now comfortably access the computer world, and technological changes are a natural part of their lives. However, they too often lose the time and space for hands-on nurturing and sharing.

We live in a fast-moving global society. There is pressure to achieve, and competition between people can be fierce. Personal relationships have suffered. People have been evaluated on what they have, rather than who they are. We have been called the 'throw-away society' which too often includes people as well as things. Our church family has been impacted by these changes–individually and corporately.

> The upheaval in families is evident everywhere in our culture. Family life is worse than it was a decade ago, and we are not sanguine about the next decade. Babies have babies, kids refuse to grow up and leave home, affluent Yuppies prize BMWs more than children, rich and poor children alike blot their minds with drugs, people casually move in with each other and out again. The divorce rate has doubled since 1965, and demographers project that half of all first marriages made today will end in divorce. Six out of ten second marriages will

probably collapse. Marriage is a fragile institution—not something anyone can count on. One third of all children born in the past decade will probably live in a stepfamily before they are eighteen. One out of every four children today is being raised by a single parent. About 22 percent of children today were born out of wedlock; of those, about a third were born to a teenage mother. One out of every five children lives in poverty; the rate is twice as high among blacks and Hispanics. [A total of] 3.4 million children live in households headed by a grandparent. In the past 25 years, the number of children in such households has increased more than 50 percent.[3]

As a result of the dramatic social forces and events of recent decades—increased sexual freedom, divorce and remarriage, out-of-wedlock births, a decline in fertility, and the rapid movement of mothers into the labor force—a range of new family structures has emerged. There are single-parent families; two-career families; blended or reconstituted families made up of couples who were married and divorced and who remarried, combining two sets of children or full-time stepchildren; and couples whose children are products of adoption, *in vivo, in vitro*, or surrogate processes. There are families consisting of homosexual couples without or with children who are biologically related to one partner or adopted; divorced homosexual parents; childless families; older divorced or married women who, for one reason or another, have assumed the parenting role to their children's children. It's a conglomerate of relationships![4]

This is not the reality "out there"; it is not "them"—it is the reality to a greater or lesser degree in each of our congregations. The reality "is us." This is a picture of our life together, the struggle of our community, the framework of our ministry, the challenge of our future. *This is our church family!*

Caring Gifts

Extending ourselves on behalf of others is a gift. As sisters we have walked paths of joy, hardship, pain, and sorrow together. We have celebrated and sustained one another. To love with our whole selves, and to have regard for each person is foundational in Jesus' teaching. He challenged us to share joy, hope, love, and peace with one another through our actions, fellowship, and testimonies. That requires respecting people for who they are, and recognizing and valuing their ideas, heritage, culture, and lifestyles. Gifts are both given and received. This is the supportive community at work.

It is a gift for all of us when we understand that our differences do not need to threaten, but when combined, expand our opportunities and enrich our lives. While we must help each other, members of a supportive family take responsibility for themselves. Each person has a service to give and a testimony to share.

The supportive congregation is there for families as they face the day-to-day life experiences of change, crisis, grief, growth, and separation. As we listen with our eyes, ears, and hearts, we can be generous in our helpfulness and cooperation. We can extend hospitality to one another and share the bounty of food, loving care, personal presence, and joyful living. We can create an environment of trust, confidence, and care that allows opportunity for forgiveness of self and each other—moving to renewal. We can celebrate one another and acknowledge gifts, achievements, and milestones—both personal and corporate. When we exemplify Christ's teachings and live them out, we *are* the caring gift.

Celebrating Life

Our church is familiar with celebratory traditions and activities. We encourage a joyful celebration in our worship. Since the beginning days of the Restoration, families have shared in potluck dinners, mid-week prayer services, vacation church schools, retreats, and reunions. These support services and activities have created opportunities for sharing our stories, recognizing the worth of all people, and listening to one another's thoughts and ideas. These are often the occasions when we slow down, take time for one another, and celebrate the gifts of life.

A variety of rich traditions and symbols is important and vital in the experience of family. Also, transitions occur regularly that bring joy and sorrow in human life. Because of these occurrences, which are held precious in individual families, they need to be celebrated and honored in the church family. The ordinary events and relationships of life need to be recognized and affirmed. This will foster connectedness within the larger household of God, will nurture spirituality, and will recognize and bless "family-ness" with one another.

Celebration of many life events and transitions can be planned into the worship calendar. The event can be part of the prelude, good news sharing, call to worship, or the focus of the entire worship service. A different Sunday can be scheduled for each celebration, or events such as birthdays and anniversaries can be grouped together. Of course, not all the celebrations would necessarily occur every year.

A small gift might be given for some of the celebrations. The people being affirmed could be invited to the front to form a circle while the pastor or another designated person offers specific prayer for the people and the occasion. Some suggestions for celebration:

- Births
- Birthdays
- Entering kindergarten
- Beginning of school year
- Blessings/Baptisms/ Confirmations
- Driver's license
- Graduation
- Marriage
- Anniversaries
- New members in congregation
- Retirement
- Remembrance of those who have died

Coming Together as the Family of God: A Vision

In the 1980s, a Peace Forum was held at the Kirtland Temple. Barbara Green, a presenter, quoted:

> . . . a family demonstrates affection, shares power and responsibility, resolves conflicts, responds to hostility, copes with illness and injury, expresses grief, encourages achievement, conducts its common meals, spends time and money, plans its vacation and travel, forms its political opinions, confronts fears for the future, and worships, or fails to worship God . . . these [actions] make the family the potential greenhouse of all peacemaking.[5]

We are connected by our rich heritage. We know where and from whom we've come. We are supported by a legacy of church history and by the individual histories we each bring to the body. We are connected by what we learn, do, and experience together in ministry and service. We need to push ahead, question, and grow together. We must connect the individual strands of each of us so that we may grow stronger and stronger.

Our congregations can be places for blending theology and heart and for feeling the Spirit. The supportive family deserves the investment of our lives. We are always more effective together than when we are separate. When we work with each other, we experience our mutual goodness, and the grace of God is set free among us.

The congregation is a place where each person and family can bring their love and find greater love in the sharing of life.

It is a place where each can celebrate life and blessing and find more fulfilling life in the celebrating with all.

It is a place where God can be encountered with questions, doubt, and faith—borrowed from each other and taken in to form a unique understanding.

It is a place where individual and family achievements, sorrows, changes, griefs, and joys can be announced, acclaimed, and remembered.

It is a place where the Sacred can be experienced in each other and in the love that is presence.

It is a place where the grace of God flows freely, uniting, bonding, and freeing.

It is a place where we will look at each other and into each other's eyes and call each other by name: sister, brother, heart friend.

It is a place where we will be understood, heard, celebrated, affirmed, and held.

It is a place where all living things will be seen as precious and holy.

It is a place where rejoicing will happen at any moment and be honored with balloons, hallelujahs, amens.

Why? Because the local congregation is the place where we are formed in Christ. It is the place where we can bring who we are as an individual or a family, and in encountering each other, blending with each other, proclaim that we are so much more and we are enough to be the family of God.

Our loving God,
You call us into family
to share our pain
to rejoice in joy
to teach the bounty of love.
Help us give ourselves, as family
to those who are lonely
to those in pain
to those whose lives
are without joy
to those who have not known
the bounty of love.
Amen.[6]

Whether we are one or many, our families are part of the children in the household of God. We are not alone or isolated. We are connected and supported, and each of us has a place in Christ's community. *Blest be the tie that binds our hearts in Christian love . . . .*

Study Questions

1. The traditional image of a family is being changed by societal forces. What is the variety of "family" arrangements in your congregation? Include members and immediate relations of members who do not attend. Make a list.
2. Ask members of your congregation—vary the ages—to write their story of a special experience when they received care from their congregational family. Build a Sunday morning service around these stories. At the conclusion of that service, allow ten minutes for each person to complete a "survey" form. The form should ask them to describe some particular need for caring by another congregation member of which they are aware. Perhaps they may also list a need of their own.
3. How literally should we take Jesus' words, "This is my commandment, that you love one another as I have loved you?" Do we treat this statement as a nice platitude, or with some serious intent? What does it mean for the actions we or our congregations take?
4. Revise the ideas for incorporating "life celebrations/recognitions" into your congregational worship. Pick two or three that can be done in the next two months at your Sunday morning service. The suggestion is to do more than simply using the recognitions as an announcement. Try to integrate them into the worship service. Brainstorm with your congregation or worship commission about other ways this can be accomplished.
5. Take time to "vision" with your congregation about being a supportive family. Imagine the characteristics of your congregation in ten years: size, services, worships, classes, community outreach, etc. Write these down, and begin creating a plan of action. List the ones you can do in one month, in six months, two years, and beyond.

6. Create the words for a love song for your congregation. Have the class describe, in a series of one-line phrases, what your ideal congregation would be like and the ways people will relate to each other. Look for opportunities to use all or portions of this "song" in future services.

Notes

1. Fred Rogers, *Peacemaking in the Family by Mister Rogers: Four Intergenerational Events for Your Church* (New York: Presbyterian Peacemaking Program, n.d.), 45.
2. Barbara Howard, *Be Swift to Love* (Independence, Missouri: Herald House), 21.
3. "The 21st Century Family: Who We Will Be—How We Will Live" *Newsweek: A Special Edition* (1995): 16.
4. Dr. Lee Salk, *Familyhood* (New York: Simon & Schuster), 21–22.
5. *The United Methodist Bishop's Foundation Document, The Manuscript Copy* (The United Methodist Church), Part IV, Sect. C, 77.
6. Tara Seeley, "Family," *Alive Now* (May/June 1992): 61.